Dear Peter,
Enjoy these clev...
rhymes of Poetry. ...
enjoyed the poetry readen...
Wickenburg this holiday season.

Love
Jerry & Earlene
12/1999

Collector's limited edition

2,000 numbered registered copies

This copy is number ___ 0349 ___

# Cowboy Poetry

## Classic Rhymes by
## Henry Herbert Knibbs
## (1874-1945)

Compiled by Mason and Janice Coggin

Cowboy
Miner
PRODUCTIONS

*Cowboy Poetry, Classic Rhymes by Henry Herbert Knibbs* (1874–1945)
Copyright © 1999 Mason and Janice Coggin
Compiled by Mason and Janice Coggin and Jon Richins
Publisher:
    Cowboy Miner Productions
    P.O. Box 9674
    Phoenix, AZ 85068
    Phone: (602) 944-3763
Seventeen poems are reprinted from *Songs of the Lost Frontier*.

### Publisher's Cataloging-in-Publication Data

Knibbs, Henry Herbert 1874–1945.
Cowboy Poetry : Classic rhymes by Henry Herbert Knibbs / Henry
    Herbert Knibbs. Compiled by Mason and Janice Coggin
        p. cm.

    ISBN: 0-9662091-1-7

1. Cowboy—Poetry. 2. Ranch life—Poetry. 3. West (U.S.)—Poetry
    I. Title
    Library of Congress Catalog Card Number: 99-64727

*Book Design & Typesetting:* SageBrush Publications, Tempe, Arizona
*Jacket Design:* ATG Productions, Christy A. Moeller, Phoenix, Arizona
*Printing:* Bang Printing, Brainerd, Minnesota
Printed and bound in the United States of America

Produced with the assistance of Dallywelter Press

Dallywelter Press
Great Falls High School Rodeo Club
Great Falls High School
Great Falls, Montana

# Acknowledgments

Without the aid of Tom Sharpe and his wife Ronna Lee, this book would have been years in production. They offered as foreword an essay they wrote for "Cowboy Poets & Cowboy Poetry," and then worked to reduce the article from sixteen pages to twelve pages to fit this book. We often turned to Tom with questions on Knibbs' life and his poetry.

Both Knibbs pictures are from the collection of Tom and Ronna Lee. Tom also offered the use of his six books of Knibbs poems to help us determine which poems to use. Several reciters of Knibbs poetry suggested that we use some of his hobo and seafaring poems. We would have liked to, but felt we needed to stay within the subject of cowboy poetry.

Jeff Streeby, faculty advisor, and Dallywelter Press, the campus press of the Great Falls High School Rodeo Club of Great Falls, Montana, are responsible for scanning the cowboy poems from the Knibbs books that are in public domain. Jeff Evenson, a senior at Great Falls High School, spent hours scanning and correcting the copy before sending it by disk to us; therefore, he definitely deserves the title of "Production Assistant."

A big thank you goes to John Schaffner for allowing us to offer for sale his tapes featuring Knibbs' poetry as well as poetry by S. Omar Barker and Badger Clark. Either tape is definitely a great companion to the book.

Our thanks also go to Waddie Mitchell, Dolan Ellis, Red Steagall and Vess Quinlan for their endorsements, and to many of our friends across the United States who have encouraged us to put together this book on the poetry of Henry Herbert Knibbs.

# Contents

# Foreword
# A Boy I Knew: A Study of
# Henry Herbert Knibbs

*Adapted from the essay by Ronna Lee and Tom Sharpe as printed in "Cowboy Poets & Cowboy Poetry," edited by David Stanley and Elaine Thatcher, Copyright 2000 by Board of Trustees of the University of Illinois.*

"**I** too knew a boy. Though he was ailing and slender and gray then, and in the grip of his last illness, he would often grin at me from his pillow, and that grin would bridge more than sixty years and he was once again the boy who had yearned over old man Howarth's violin."[1]

Though he never earned a dime as a cowboy, Henry Herbert Knibbs (1874-1945) was known for his writing of western stories, novels, screenplays and poems, with his forte being the poems. A few of these poems were remembered by the working cowboys[2] and passed in verse and song along the trails. The remembered poems tended to be quite humorous, though his better writing was serious. Most of his writing fell through the cracks and disappeared until the recent resurrection[3] of cowboy poetry, when the search for something new, or old and forgotten rekindled the interest in Knibbs' work.

---

1   Editor's Farewell written by Turbesé Lummis for the unpublished manuscript of *A Boy I Knew* the autobiography of Henry Herbert Knibbs' childhood.

2   Keith Lummis, friend of Henry Herbert Knibbs, son of Charles F. Lummis, and brother of Turbesé Lummis Fiske, as told to Ronna Lee and Tom Sharpe in an interview September, 1991.

3   Cowboy poetry never really died, but like the cowboy, you just couldn't see it from the interstate.

It is not often that writings by non-cowboys are accepted. Harry Knibbs, however, spent a lot of time traveling in the Southwest learning the language and the ways of those who lived there. His original intention in this study was to be able to duplicate the authenticity of locale written by his friend Eugene Manlove Rhodes, who was a cowboy and rancher of some stature in southwest New Mexico in the late 1800s. Knibbs had met Rhodes while Knibbs was working for the B. R. & P. Railroad in the east. This study and Knibbs' ability to paint with words makes him one of the sought after and accepted classic poets.

It is unusual to attend a classics session at a cowboy poetry gathering today and not be treated to at least one poem written by Knibbs. It might be the camp cook humor of "Boomer Johnson" that has been passed from campfire to campfire by generations of working cowboys, or it might be the lilting beauty and sensitivity of "Where The Ponies Come To Drink," that brings tears to the eye of the philosopher as well as the grizzled cowhand!

In his seventy years, Knibbs told hundreds of stories. His novels, screenplays, poems and short stories explored many topics and tapped every emotion. Perhaps the most moving story of all was the one he began to tell at the end of his life. Knibbs' unpublished autobiography, *A Boy I Knew*, is a fine piece of writing. Part personal memoir, rich in facts about his childhood, it also holds the key to understanding the origins, the popularity and the tragedy of the career-ending mistake made by the once-popular, recently rediscovered Western writer. Details of Knibbs' life story gathered from published biographical sketches, his personal and professional papers, interviews with his close personal friends, and his own reminiscences, provide some context in which to interpret Knibbs' ability to write so effectively about Western life.

The small town of Clifton, Ontario, Canada (later known as Niagara Falls) seems an unlikely birthplace for a Western writer. Nevertheless, it was there that Henry Herbert Knibbs was born, on October 24, 1874, to his American parents, Sara and George. His childhood revolved around several factors that would deeply influence his later life and work—adventure, curiosity and independence, family, poetry, horses and "Fiddle."

By the time he was five years old, Harry[4] had already become preoccupied with a violin. He had noticed a beautiful instrument in a shop window but had never heard one's voice. At a memorable Church Garden Party, however, " . . . the boy even forgot the ice cream when Mr. Colethurst began to play his violin. Just how well he played, the boy never knew. But even today, his spine can still feel the thrill that went up it when he first heard the sound of Mr. Colethurst's violin."[5]

With new admiration, the boy gazed at the violin in Howarth's window, for he had learned that It wasn't just a fancy box made of wood. It was a passport to another world. Still wearing short dresses, Harry craved to own the violin. Unfortunately, his life's savings, stored in an old cowhide trunk in the woodshed, totaled considerably less than half the stiff purchase price of $3.50. He devised several schemes to amass the fortune. Some were brilliant, some less than honest, and most made for intriguing stories. The strain of acquiring and saving nickels, dimes and quarters without his parents' knowledge or consent and the fear that his prize would be snapped up by someone else "used up a lot of boy."

At last, lacking only 25 cents, he visited his father at the bank and asked for the additional money to buy something special. Father asked off-handedly if he planned to buy a horse. Henry replied, "No, it's not that big."

Harry now had the fiddle, but dared not play it, for the instrument was too precious to suffer at his unskilled hand. He also feared discovery and imagined the forced return of the unnecessary luxury to Howarth's shop. Harry kept "Fiddle"

---

4    Henry's friends called him Harry.
5    The unpublished manuscript of *A Boy I Knew*, the autobiography of Henry Herbert Knibbs' childhood. All quotations are from this manuscript, unless otherwise noted.

11

hidden in the woodshed, safely tucked away in the same cowhide trunk where he had hidden his coins, taking it out only to hold, admire and pet.

When at last he overcame his fears and put bow to string he was overheard. It was the groom across the street who first discovered Harry's secret. At the groom's request, Harry reluctantly handed over the fiddle and was amazed as the sweet sound of "Sailor's Hornpipe" flew from the strings. Jarvey the roustabout, who fed horses and shoveled manure for a living, had become a person of influence. He could play the violin!

Jarvey demonstrated the playing of fifths and was the first to teach Harry "to hear—actually hear—the voice" of his violin. "Each day Fiddle meant more to me. It wasn't just a varnished box with four strings. It was something alive and filled with voices. Occasionally, it would sing."

Eventually George and Sara discovered not only the fiddle but also their son's passion for it. "Fiddle" was moved from the cowhide trunk to a place of honor beneath his bed, but until winter arrived, Harry's practicing was limited to the woodshed "studio." Formal lessons proved to be of some value, but Harry continued to rely on his ear and his instinct—"something told me inside when the fiddle sounded right."

He heard, played and owned many fine fiddles and finally operated the Farthing Hub Violin Shop in Banning, California. How could there not be music in the poetry of this man who, at the age of seven, had a best friend named "Fiddle"?

Despite his mischievous streak, Knibbs remembered his family with fondness and reverence. Even the arrival of a baby sister, though viewed at the time with some skepticism, was remembered with humor. "I thought that life was just right. It never occurred to me that it could change. And then my baby sister was born . . . . Some people never think about earthquakes happening to *them*. I had never thought much about babies. And now one had happened to me."

Harry's love and respect for his family is portrayed in the following passage that describes his punishment for stealing fifty cents for his fiddle fund from their hired girl's purse.

"But to be sent upstairs to bed, not alone supperless, but deprived of the warm feeling of companionship and well-being you had when you sat at the supper table with your father and mother, hungry for the food which smelled so good, and unaware that you hungered quite as much for love and sympathy and understanding— and praise if you had earned it; when you eagerly unburdened your heart of the day's triumphs and failures (omitting to mention little indiscretions and mistakes), and your mother was going to read to you after the supper things had been cleared away and you had done your lessons; to be deprived of all this, to show that you were in disgrace, an outcast whom your father and mother no longer loved, was a punishment so bitter you felt you could never survive it."

For the most part, though, he remembered that "Mother was an Angel and Father and I were chums." George Knibbs was a senior clerk at Pierce, Howard and Company, Bankers in Niagara Falls. After the company quit the banking business to concentrate on the coal industry, George became a full partner. The business eventually failed, leaving the comfortable family in financial trouble.

Knibbs credited his early exposure to and appreciation of poetry to his father. "How many of the grace notes of existence I owe to my father! His sprightliness could lift the dullest hour to a frolic. The works of Longfellow, Lord Byron, Whittier, Tennyson, Edgar Allen Poe and other popular poets gave father a chance to disport himself for the amusement of the family." Harry's father, the son of a man with little formal education, endowed Harry with valuable qualities including politeness, gentility and a sense of humor.

It was Wib, the hired man on his grandparents' farm who first taught young Harry about the power of language. "He had a dry ornate way of talking that was fascinating to a small boy, and his admonitions were a great deal more impressive to me than if he had used ordinary country language. When he told me that Grandmothers' fields and pasture lots were 'densely populated with rattlesnakes,' it really made me want to watch out where I was going, when an ordinary grownup warning would have sounded like a lecture and put my country back up."

In a chapter he titled "My Grandma was a Thoroughbred" Knibbs notes that "The man who hasn't spent at least a portion of his boyhood on a farm has missed the best part of his life." Harry spent every summer vacation of his first fifteen years on his grandparent's Pennsylvania farm. Between ages one and five, he was escorted there by his mother. "When I was five years old, father took me to the station, fastened a tag on my coat lapel, put me on the Erie train, and shipped me to Grandmother's all by myself." During these childhood train rides, Harry became increasingly independent and fond of travel. He dreamed of becoming a railroad conductor and did in fact spend some time later in life as a hobo. At Grandma's farm Harry became acquainted with his extended family and acquired a great respect for his ancestors' pioneer spirit and hard work.

Like his poetry, Knibbs' recounting of childhood farm memories is characterized by deep emotion, acute observation, and detailed description. "It is more than half a hundred years since I last saw the old farm. The family has long since scattered; most have died. But I have not forgotten one little corner of Grandmother's place."

"I can seem to see every fence post and clump of petunias. I can see Grandma herself, now rosy with vexation at some misdeed of that dratted boy, now beaming with the loving kindness her heart was full of. I am glad to keep such memories in that one spot where they will never fade."

Harry cultivated his second love during summers spent on Grandmother's farm. "Of course fiddles were the most important things in the world. Except when I was looking at horses." In a chapter entitled "Fiddle and Four Legs," Knibbs' autobiography explores his love, respect and understanding of horses and their relationship to people. This aspect of Knibbs' early years helps to explain his ability to speak so well through his later poetry to the cowboy and horseman.

He couldn't pinpoint the exact moment when he "first loved horses" but he suspected "it was probably the first time I ever saw one." It was in his blood "to love fine horses" for his Pennsylvania relatives were not only farmers and teachers, but also horsemen and breeders. Great Uncle Smith bred horses, and Aunt Lib "was the only person, man or woman, who could handle Frank, her beautiful black gelding." "I liked Aunt Lib!" Of his Grandmother he said, "If I hadn't admired her for anything else, I would have had to admire her for the way she had with horses. Grandmother was a notable horsewoman. I shall never forget the authority, the daring, and the good hard sense with which she handled her favorite mare."

"Even when I was in short dresses whenever there was a fence with a horse on one side of it, you could see me on the other peering as close as I could get to see all there was to see. And when I graduated to short pants I spent my time in Uncle Smith's barn whenever I could, pestering the hired men when they hitched up or fetched in the work teams. I wanted to help unharness. I wanted to feed and water the horses. I wanted to do everything but keep out of the way when the men were working around the horses. I'm surprised I didn't ask to sleep with them."

Occasionally, Henry was allowed to ride on the "front seat of a hack driver's carriage" and he wanted nothing more than to grow up quickly, have his own horses and buggies and go into business as a hack driver. From this perfect observation point he was able to note each and every detail of the horses' actions, and he stored the scene away in his exceptional memory. Several decades later he called upon his remarkable skill to fashion vivid, poetic images from those detailed memories.

"I could see all around and I could see the backs of Tom Riley's horses gently move up and down like the shafts of our sewing machine. I could watch what they did with their heads and keep track of their ears. I loved to see how those ears moved, like little men, stood still, listened, moved sidewards or forwards again."

Ironically, it would be one of his two boyhood passions that caused his demise as a writer. An error in a published short story involving a misstatement of a biological fact about horses, would bring an abrupt end to a successful, varied and then tragically-ended writing career.

From his family and farm experiences during the first fifth of his life, Knibbs gained a great deal of useful knowledge and a keen intuition about people as well as horses. "There on the farm I could see with my own eyes what it meant to breed a strain for courage, endurance and spirit. Gradually, I came to see that it applied just as well to people as horses." Armed with these insights, a spirit of adventure, an unquenchable thirst for knowledge, and a love of horses, poetry and fiddles, he was ready to embark upon adulthood.

Though Henry Herbert Knibbs never did graduate from college, he was educated. He attended Woodstock College at Woodstock, Ontario at the age of 14, and Bishop Ridley College at St. Catherine's, Ontario at the age of 15, spending three years there. He also studied English at Harvard for three years. Upon leaving Bishop Ridley College, at age 18, Knibbs migrated to Buffalo, New York and found employment as a wholesale coal salesman with a Michigan/Ontario territory. He left there to clerk at the Lehigh Valley Railroad office.

A short time later, he took off for a two-year stint as a hobo in the Middle West. Completing this tour, he married and went to work as a stenographer in the Division Freight Office of the B. R. P. Railway in Buffalo, New York. When he was summoned to the Rochester Office to become a private secretary to the traffic manager, he built a house but never lived in it. He decided at the age of thirty four, it was time to go to Harvard.

Three years later, in 1910, at the age of thirty seven, he moved to California and wrote his first Western Novel, *Lost Farm Camp*. When it was published, he took off on an extensive trip through the Southwestern states of New Mexico, California and Arizona trying to duplicate the accuracy of locale that he admired in Eugene Manlove Rhodes' writing. He studied hard in his travels, learning enough about the West to be considered an authority on it, and he became highly respected by his fellow Western writers.

In 1899, Knibbs had married Ida Julia Phiefer. Thirty years later he left Ida to live with Turbesé Lummis Fiske whose father he had known before he left the East. Ida refused to divorce Harry and wrote to him daily for the first year, then weekly, and eventually annually begging him to return and denouncing the woman with whom he was living. The reasons for the separation are very speculative.

Born June 8, 1892, Turbesé Lummis was the daughter of Charles Lummis, editor and writer of Western stories. Turbesé was very influential in Knibbs' later years. After Knibbs left his wife, he moved in with Turbesé, who for some unknown reason was no longer living with her husband, a Mr. Fiske. Turbesé and Knibbs conspired to write a novel together and she edited a lot of his work including his autobiography, which she attempted several times to get published. As a side note, after Knibbs' death, Ida went to court to gain the copyrights owned by Henry and claimed by Turbesé. Ida lost.

Among the people Knibbs associated with was Charles Lummis, father of Turbesé, whom he had met before he moved to California. Frank King, a writer for the *Western Livestock Journal*, became his friend and introduced the name of Bruce Kiskaddon to Knibbs, though it is unknown whether or not they ever met or corresponded. Like Charles Lummis, Eugene Manlove Rhodes had become a friend of Knibbs before he left for the West. At one point the friendship between them became quite strained when Knibbs used Rhodes as a character in *The Ridin' Kid from Powder River*. Knibbs more than made up for this in his novel *Partners of Chance* where the hero was based completely on Rhodes.[6]

Harry wrote six books of poems. The first, aptly titled *First Poems*, had three hundred copies published, all signed and numbered. This book was published under the pen name of Henry K. Herbert. The remaining five books were written with a less formal more familiar style. The pictures he painted with words can put the reader right into the scene. You sit at the table when the cow waddie punches "Boomer Johnson" and you can smell the pines in "Where The Ponies Come To Drink." The topics of these poems take you from the sea to the plains and through the mountains both on horseback and on foot with the stars and dogs for companions. Knibbs' books of poems include:

1. *First Poems*, Rochester, New York, The Geneses Press, 1908
2. *Songs of the Outlands: Ballads of the Hoboes and Other Verse*, Boston, Houghton Mifflin, 1914
3. *Riders of the Stars: A Book of Western Verse*, Boston, Houghton Mifflin, 1916
4. *Songs of the Trail*, Boston, Houghton Mifflin, 1920
5. *Saddle Songs and Other Verse*, Boston, Houghton Mifflin, 1922
6. *Songs of the Lost Frontier*, Boston, Houghton Mifflin, 1930

Knibbs was the author of thirteen novels, considered by most to be somewhat lacking in theme. He always seemed to allow the bad guy to win, and the heroine always ran off with the hero. He often included a character who was a wanderer and had a violin. His pictures of the Southwest were quite good.

Knibbs wrote for various pulp magazines of the time, including *Saturday Evening Post*, *Red Cross Magazine*, *Current Opinion*, *West*, *Western Stories* and *Adventure*, just to name a

---

6    *Encyclopedia of Frontier and Western Fiction*, Jon Tuska and Vicki Piekarski, Editors in Chief, McGraw-Hill Book Company

few. Some of these submissions were poems and others were stories. Most of his novels were printed serially before they were combined and bound into book form.

Being a writer of the West in the early part of this century, Knibbs was closely watched by his contemporaries. In a series of short stories for the *Saturday Evening Post* about a horse called *Pericles,* he inadvertently quoted the gestation period of a mare as nine months instead of eleven months. His peers completely defamed him for this error. It was a shocking blow to the writer. He tried many times to explain the error for he knew the correct term, but the damage was done, and none of his stories were ever again accepted for publication.

Knibbs turned back to his first love, "Fiddle," and spent his remaining years running the violin shop in Banning, California. "Certain words can be ridden like horses. One word carries me farther than any horse has ever done. That word is violin."

The only writing of much consequence in the last few years of Knibbs' life was the autobiographical manuscript, which remains unpublished and mostly unknown to this day. It will be a great loss if *A Boy I Knew,* remains unpublished, for captured within its nearly three hundred typewritten pages are some of the finest examples of personal history ever written. It is the story of late nineteenth century small town life and the childhood adventures of a very special man.

On May 17, 1945, Knibbs died in California from a respiratory illness from which he had suffered most of his life.

"It was only recently that I realized I was a ticket of leave man. I rather wish I had realized it toward the beginning and not the end of my furlough."[7]

---

7    Introduction to *A Boy I Knew,* unpublished manuscript by Henry Herbert Knibbs

# The Shallows of the Ford

Did you ever wait for daylight
    when the stars along the river
Floated thick and white as snowflakes
    in the water deep and strange,
Till a whisper through the aspens
    made the current break and shiver
As the frosty edge of morning
    seemed to melt and spread and change?

Once I waited, almost wishing
    that the dawn would never find me;
Saw the sun roll up the ranges
    like the glory of the Lord;
Was about to wake my partner
    who was sleeping close behind me,
When I saw the man we wanted
    spur his pony to the ford.

Saw the ripples of the shallows
    and the muddy streaks that followed.
As the pony stumbled toward me
    in the narrows of the bend;
Saw the face I used to welcome,
    wild and watchful, lined and hollowed;
And God knows I wished to warn him,
    for I once had called him friend.

But an oath had come between us—
    I was paid by law and Order;
He was outlaw, rustler, killer—
    so the border whisper ran;
Left his word in Caliente
    that he'd cross the Rio border . . .
Call me coward? But I hailed him . . .
"Riding close to daylight, Dan!"

Just a hair and he'd have got me,
    but my voice, and not the warning,
Caught his hand and held him steady;
    then he nodded, spoke my name,
Reined his pony round and fanned it
    in the bright and silent morning,
Back across the sunlit Rio
    up the trail on which he came.

He had passed his word to cross it—
    and I had passed my word to get him—
We broke even and we knew it;
    'twas a case of give-and-take
For old times. I could have killed him
    from the brush, instead, I let him
Ride his trail. . . I turned . . . my partner
    flung his arm and stretched wake;

Saw me standing in the open;
    pulled his gun and came beside me;
Asked a question with his shoulder
    as his left hand pointed toward
Muddy streaks that thinned and vanished . . .
    not a word, but hard he eyed me
As the water cleared and sparkled
    in the shallows of the ford.

# The Fighting Parson

He was a right good man—a parson, too;
    Deep-chested, tall, and straight. He had an eye
You couldn't get away from; kind and blue,
    And wise to all it saw; just like the sky

Out here in Arizona,—always clear,
    Or mostly clear. Of course, sometimes it rained;
But if the fighting parson shed a tear,
    The peace he lost, some other fellow gained.

The parson sometimes had to use his hands,
    And save his wind to finish up a fight.
He didn't just stand up and give commands
    In settling what was wrong and what was right;

He backed his words in good two-fisted style,
    And never quit until the job was done.
Yes, he could shoot and ride, get licked, and smile
    As easy after as when he begun.

But mighty few could handle him, at that;
    He was all man—religion, it came next.
If talking wouldn't do, off came his hat
    And coat—and then his double-barreled text.

Once he got licked—the only time I know.
    It kind of scared us, seeing him go down,
Dropped by a lightning smash from Placer Joe
    Who just rode in to salivate the town.

"If that's the best you got," said Placer Joe,
    "Go rope a real one somewhere." No one spoke
Until the fighting parson, rising slow,
    Brushed off his clothes, just like it was a joke;

"No, not the best," he said, "and not the worst;
    Perhaps I was mistaken in my plan;
We'll try again, but let me tell you first,
    You haven't whipped religion; just a man.

"What if I'm whipped again? That's not the end.
    What if you kill me and my spirit sped
Up to my Master? Let me tell you, friend,
    He'll send as good, or better, in my stead."

That staggered Joe. He hadn't thought of that;
    And something seemed to kill his wish to fight.
He grinned and fumbled foolish with his hat,
    And said, "By Gosh, I guess the parson's right!"

The parson wasn't licked, at that, but hid
    The knock-down—having better in his hand . . .
They made him Bishop, sir, and when they did,
    We lost the finest parson in the land.

## Rain-Makers

Where the rattler coils in the yucca shade
    and the lizard's hue is bright,
Where the riven sandstone holds the heat
    through the hours of the desert night,
South and South of the Hopi line—
    South of the Navajo,
The shattered walls of a ruin stand—
    a village of long ago.

A puncher seeking a water-hole
    that his thirsty horse might drink,
Reined to the edge of the salt-white glare
    on the rim of a desert sink,
Gazed at the ruins banked with sand
    as he topped a rounded rise,
And a vision of ancient Hopi Land
    grew clear in his steady eyes.

The arrowhead, the painted shard,
   and the ash of a vanished flame;
Roofs long fallen that choked the rooms—
   a village without a name. . .
He thought of the hopes and joys and fears
   that this patient people knew,
Lost in the vagrant sweep of years,
   believing their gods were true.

"They prayed for rain," the puncher said,
   "and I reckon if I knew how,
I'd rustle a little prayer myself,
   for we sure need rain right now;
And here are the deer and turkey bones
   which shows that they liked their meat,
And here are some busted grinding-stones
   for the corn they used to eat."

Then he found a bead, a turquoise bead,
   blue bright on the littered sand,
And he pictured a dusky Hopi girl,
   a beauty of Hopi Land,
When the long-dry cañon river-bed was cool
   with a crystal flow,
And she swayed to the brimming olla's weight
   on the foot-worn trail below.

What if the puncher went to sleep
   in the shade of the ruin wall,
While his pony dozed in the noonday sun
   with the blue sky over all?
What if he saw the Hopi folk
   do a primitive rain-prayer dance,
With symbol of turtle, snake and gourd
   and the lightning's broken lance?

Then the far hills shouldered a thunder-head,
    the light grew dim and strange,
A shaft of blue went hurtling through
    and echoed from range to range;
The puncher opened his sleepy eyes
    and gazed at the distant plain,
A storm-black line on the desert rim,
    and the welcome tang of rain.

He thought of his homestead down the creek
    and the cracked and thirsty earth,
He thought of his cattle, gaunt and weak
    in the season's drought and dearth;
The withered truck in his garden-patch
    that fought with the summer heat,
As he sniffed the rain, the saving rain,
    and its smell was cool and sweet.

Snug in his shack he made a fire,
    had supper and rolled a smoke,
Doorway open he viewed the storm
    and visioned the Hopi folk . . . .
Searched his pockets to find a match
    and found in his hand instead,
The thin, blue ring of a turquoise bead
    and a jet-black arrowhead.

# The Edge of Town

The scattering sage stands thin and tense
As though afraid of the barbed-wire fence;
A windmill purrs in the lazy breeze
And a mocker sings in the pepper trees,
And beneath their shadows, gold and blue,
Hangs the old red olla, rimmed with dew:
Where the valley quail in the twilight call,
As the sunset fades on the 'dobe wall,
Just where the foothill trail comes down,
I have made my home on the edge of town.

A few green acres fenced and neat,
By a road that will never become a street;
And once in a while, down the dusty way
A traveler comes at the end of day;
A desert rat or some outland tramp,
Seeking a place for his evening camp;
The door of my 'dobe is four feet wide,
And there's always a bed and a meal, inside.

And many a one of the wights that roam,
Has stopped at my house and found a home:
And many a tale of these outland folk
Has furnished a tang to the evening smoke,
While the stars shone down on our dwelling-place,
And the moon peered in at a dusky face.

Singers, they, of the open land;
The timbered peak and the desert sand,
Peril and joy of the hardy quest,
Trail and pack of the unspoiled West:
Though crowded back to the lone, last range,
Their dream survives that will never change.

When the hill-stream roars from the far-off height,
And the rain on the patio dances white;
When the log in my winter fireplace gleams,
And my Airedale whimpers his hunting-dreams;
Should a boot-heel grate on the portal floor,
Should I hear a knock at the dripping door,
Then I know that romance has again come down
From the high, far hills, to the edge of town.

# The Wind

The wind marched down the cañon
    with the lightnings in his hand;
He thrust the trees aside
    as he let the lightnings ride
When he loosed them
    where the dripping walls below Chilao stand.

He tore the autumn music
    from the cottonwoods of gold
In the hunger of his march
    from each cloudy arch to arch:
His silver horses spurned the black
    that down the cañon rolled.

He struck the sullen water;
    choked the pool with blinding leaves:
His fingers, edged with white,
    raked the stars from out the night:
He filled and tilted overside
    the heavens' flooded eaves.

Then he bent his head and listened,
    and the listeners grew still:
The huddled quail a-quiver
    in the thicket by the river,
The buck that stamped and trembled
    on the trail along the hill:
The rabbit in the aspens
    and the fox among the fern,
And the rattler on the ridges
    where the manzanitas burn.

Then he smote the drum of Silence
    as he rose from off his knees,
Shook the rain from out his eyes,
    shook the rafters of the skies,
Fluted music of the giants
    in the hollows of the trees,
Droned a dirge along the mountain
    where the stunted timber dies.

Strode untrammeled through the Narrows,
    matched his thunder with their own:
Ripped the rotting log asunder,
    drew the flotsam down and under,
Stooped and thrust his lusty shoulder
    to the rocking river stone;
Cast the stinging spray before him
    as he marched along, alone.

Jose de la Crux Y' Barra,
    of Tejunga and the vine,
Crossed himself in sudden dread
    as he cowered in his bed,
Then he shivered to the table
    and he poured a glass of wine;
The ruddy embers flickered
    and the floating ashes fled,
Fluttered softly in the shadows,
    settled softly on his head—
As the wind drew wild staccato
    from the shingle and the door,
And the creeping ghost of Winter
    creaked and chattered on the floor.

Deep and dead the moon lay strangled
    in the meshes of a cloud,
And the hoofs of silver horses
    struck a flame along the land:
Struck the cabin of Y' Barra—
    and the wind he flung a shroud:
Shook the granite with his tread
    as he tramped along the sand,
Marched from out the midnight cañon
    with the lightnings in his hand.

# The Rancho in the Rain

The rabbit's ears are flattened
    and he's squattin' scared and still,
Ag'inst the drippin' cedar;
    and the quail below the hill
Are huddled up together
    where the brush is close and thick;
The snow is meltin' on the range
    And chokin' up the creek;
The clouds are hangin' level,
    draggin' slow across the plain,
And me? I'm settin'
    smokin' and a-smilin' at the rain.

There's a saddle that needs mendin'
    and some overalls that's tore;
But the stock is fed and happy
    and the milk is on the shelf.
Now a woman would raise ructions
    at the mud that's on the floor,
But it's rainin' on the rancho—
    and I'm runnin' things myself.

Kind of lonesome? Well, for some folks,
    but I'm used to livin' so;
If I feel the need of talkin',
    There's the puppy and his pranks:
There's the hosses in the stable,
    munchin' easy-like and slow,
And it's company to feed 'em
    and to hear 'em nicker thanks.

With my feet ag'inst the fender
    and the fire a-snappin' bright,
And the smell of burnin' cedar
    mixin' pleasant with my smoke,
And a-r'arin', tearin' story of the range,
    That's ribbed up right,
Why lay off and fix the damper
    when the isinglass is broke?

I'm a-bachin'; that's the answer;
    takin' orders jest from me,
And I aim to say I'm workin'
    for a kind of friendly boss,
Not forgettin' there's the Master
    That's a-talyin' to see
If I'm hangin' with the drags
    or puttin' every deal across.

Kind of simple, this here livin',
    if a fella keeps his head,
Keeps the stock from gittin' ribby,
    keeps his fences tight and straight,
Sweats enough to keep him limber,
    ain't afraid to go to bed
When the boys are up and drinkin',
    playin' cards, and settin' late.

Ridin' range and punchin' cattle,
    I've took notice now and then,
That the man who's fair to critters
    is the kind to reach the top;
He'll be workin' willin' hosses
    and be workin' willin' men,
But no man is savin' money
    that will spur 'em till they drop.

But it's *rainin'*—jest a-roarin';
   and the desert's drinkin' deep;
On the bunk-house roof
   the water's talkin' sassy-like and bold,
And the world she looks as if
   She'd kind of like to go to sleep,
But the rain it sure won't let her—
   keeps her shiverin' and cold.

Here comes Buddy crost the pasture,
   buttin' weather strong and stout;
Now I wonder what's the racket?
   Yearlin' bogged at Mesa Lake!
Hunt the stove—I'll git my slicker.
   And you couldn't git her out?
Well, I reckon we can make it.
   I'll jest saddle up Old Jake.
. . . . . . . . . . . . . . . . . . . . . . . . . . .
That's the way it goes with ranchin'—
   never know what's goin' to come:
Luck or trouble, till it hits you,
   so you got to guess it, some.

Saved that yearlin'. Mud and leather!
   But the fire feels good ag'in!
Yes, you got to keep a-guessin'
   and you'll hit it, now and then.
Night has stitched the clouds together,
   but she's left a hole or two,
And a mighty slimsy linin'
   where the water's pourin' through,
But it's feedin' thirsty pasture,
   makin' hay and makin' grain,
And I'm settin' warm—and smokin'—
   and a-smilin' at the rain.

# The Reata

Fernando slowly plaited close
 the long, strong rawhide strands;
Inch by inch the stout reata grew
 beneath his horny hands;
As he sang a Spanish love-song—
 sang until his work was done,
Knotted in the woven honda,
 when the shadow of his son,
Young Miguel, crossed to the patio,
 paused and stood beside his sire,
And the new, smooth-coiled reata
 filled his heart with keen desire.

Old Fernando took the olla
 from the shadowy pepper-tree,
Drank the fresh, cool water slowly,
 sighed and most contentedly
Rolled a cigarette and smoked it—
 blew a ring within a ring,
Said: "You like the new reata?
 It is yours, if you will sing
That old song your madre taught you;
 song and singer, years ago
Silent . . ." Then the old song in the sunlit patio:

 "More swift am I than the flash of wings!
 Stronger am I than steel!
 Luck to the hand that my fleet coil flings,
 Mine is the song that my master sings,
 Rounding me reel on reel.

"What of the herd were it not for me,
The reata, lithe and light?
What of the horses that break and flee
To the hills in the starry night?

"Swift they may flee, but the swifter I
Leap to the running steer,
Or loop a foot as the ponies fly,
When ye may not come as near.

"I, the reata, fold on fold,
Coiled and uncoiled again;
Swift as the serpent to strike—and hold
In the dust of the branding-pen.

"Yea, you may jingle your bright bell spur,
Your conchas like stars may shine,
As you proudly ride past the eyes of her . . .
But the soul of it all is mine.

"For I earn the gold;
with the same ye buy
Saddle, serape, spur,
Sombrero and steed, but the king am I,
As ye ride past the eyes of her."

Old Fernando Ruiz wove it,
    drawing close the rawhide strands,
Inch by inch the stout reata grew
    beneath his horny hands:
With a song Miguel had won it;
    with a song he rode away,
While Fernando in the shadows
    dreamed of faces brave and gay.

## Benny Benito

W ho found him encountered a rugged decline,
　　To a far, sunny valley, and fronting his field,
Corral and adobe, neat garden and vine,
　　Beans, chili, and melons—a bountiful yield.

His door ever open to any who came,
　　And his welcome, though mixed, was politely complete:
"*Buenos dias!* You hongry? Benito my name;
　　She is *mucho calor;* I fix you the eat."

Your saddle and bridle hung up in the shack,
　　And Benny observing with humorous shrug
Your horse as he rolls, "*Si,* he scratch heem the back!"
　　Then a seat in the arbor—a tall wicker jug.

"The *vino,* I make heem. You like the good drink?
　　*Buena suerte!* I wait till those dinner I bring,
Those *frijoles,* those *queso, tortillas*—I think,
　　Yes, I fix the new fire and those coffee she sing."

When dusk, velvet-padded, swift, stealthily slips,
　　Down into the valley, and silences fill
With the fragrance of pines, and the candle flame dips,
　　To a wandering breeze drifting over the hill,

In a friendly discussion of ways and of means,
　　Benito grows eloquent, proud of his own
Independence, his burros, his melons and beans;
　　"*Si!* I make heem go good, and I make heem alone.

"When the sun she is shine on two side of the fence,
    Those *gallinas*—those chicken—she lay the good egg;
When she old, she is cook: what you say, the expense,
    Is *nada*. Oh, sometime she tough in the leg.

"Those alfalfa she grow, and those *higos*—you say,
    The fig—*Si!* I pick heem and dry heem and keep;
And those chili and onion I put heem away,
    When the winter she come and the groun' she is sleep.

"Sometime with those burro I make to the gold,
    Leetle pasear—lejos—where no *hombre* see;
She is hide in the desert. I look. She is old,
    Long time she is hide but I find the gold, me!

"*Ai! Mucho dinero* for mans she is bad,
    He no work, he go sick, and his hongry she go;
Me, I strong like the horse. And those big *soledad*,
    She is speak what you say, 'Take heem easy—go slow!'

"So *manana* I make heem, sometime, yes, I think—
    '*Pobrecito!* That old mountain-lion!' you say;
But this place she is mine, and the eat and the drink;
    And this place she is yours all the time what you stay."

# The Cowboy and the Cañon

"Some Titan showed his anger when he made
    That mark upon the world," the poet said.
A cowboy, loafing in the cedar shade,
    Nodded and rose, "Last night I sort of strayed—
Let's get a real, wet drink; I'm right near dead!"
    The painter smiled and closed a humorous eye.
"We'll go with you, and drink, before you die."

The great cleft drew apart as down the rut
Of sand and scattered torrent rock, the three
Plodded in silence. "Some steam-shovel cut!"
The cowboy murmured, swearing soulfully.

Then suddenly the western rampart threw
A shadow in the cañon, cool and clean;
The ragged walls that hulked against the blue
Blotted the living world, while in between
Wavered three pygmies who had once been men;
The miracle of contrast burdening
Their journey with a vision-picture—when
They came upon the mystery of a spring
Flooding a hollowed rock.
                            The cowboy sank
Prone on the granite, dipped his mouth and drank.

Grunting he rose, all satisfied, and stood
With boot heel grinding in a mound of sand,.
Remarking that the drink was "mighty good!"
Rolling a cigarette with skillful hand,
He puffed content, watching the smoke rings where
They vanished wavering in the slumbering air.

The sunlight and the shadows seemed asleep;
No faintest sound awoke from rim to rim,
Save a thin trickle and the murmuring seep
Bubbling from hidden caverns cool and dim;
Till, from the barren edge against the west,
There thrilled the silvery plaint of some wee bird:
"*Dear! Dear! Dear! When shall we make the nest?*"
Then came the answer, clear as spoken word,
Out of the dusk across the cañon furled:
"*Dear! Dear! Dear! Today we make the nest!*"
And, "*Dear! Dear! Dear! How beautiful the world!*"

Back in the cow-camp jest and laughter broke
The placid level of the evening cool;
The cowboy, frying bacon, turned and spoke;
"Perhaps you guys will think that I'm a fool,
But while you swallowed that there cañon sight,
A bird got busy with his little song,
As plain as talking, and he had it right!
'*Beer! Beer! Beer! But water tastes the best!*'
I got it straight, right from the cañon crest . . . .
Here come the boys—don't tell—or I'm in wrong!"

# Punchin' Dough

Come, all you young waddies, I'll sing you a song,
Stand back from the wagon—stay where you belong:
I've heard you observin' I'm fussy and slow,
While you're punchin' cattle and I'm punchin' dough.

Now I reckon your stomach would grow to your back
If it wa'n't for the cook that keeps fillin' the slack:
With the beans in the box and the pork in the tub,
I'm a-wonderin' now, who would fill you with grub?

You think you're right handy with gun and with rope,
But I've noticed you're bashful when usin' the soap:
When you're rollin' your Bull for your brown cigarette
I' been rollin' the dough for them biscuits you et.

When you're cuttin' stock, then I'm cuttin' a steak:
When you're wranglin' hosses, I'm wranglin' a cake:
When you're hazin' the dogies and battin' your eyes,
I'm hazin' dried apples that aim to be pies.

You brag about shootin' up windows and lights,
But try shootin' biscuits for twelve appetites:
When you crawl from your roll and the ground it is froze,
Then who biles the coffee that thaws out your nose?

In the old days the punchers took just what they got:
It was sow-belly, beans, and the old coffee-pot;
But now you come howlin' for pie and for cake,
Then you cuss at the cook for a good bellyache.

You say that I'm old, with my feet on the skids;
Well, I'm tellin' you now that you're nothin' but kids:
If you reckon your mounts are some snaky and raw,
Just try ridin' herd on a stove that won't draw.

When you look at my apron, you're readin' my brand,
Four-X, which is sign for the best in the land:
On bottle or sack it sure stands for good luck,
So line up, you waddies, and wrangle your chuck.

No use of your snortin' and fightin' your head;
If you like it with chili, just eat what I said:
For I aim to be boss of this end of the show
While you're punchin' cattle, and I'm punchin' dough.

# Bread

Oh, my heart it is just achin'
    For a little bite of bacon,
  A hunk of bread, a little mug of brew;
    I'm tired of seein' scenery,
  Just lead me to a beanery
    Where there's something more than
      only air to chew.

# Bill McGee

Oh, Bill McGee he was long and lean
    with a couple of miles of thirst,
His talk was tough and his eye was mean—
    that is, when you met him first;
But that was only a way he had of making
    a stranger stare,
For Bill was anything else but bad,
    and square as a die is square.

"When Bill falls down he is halfway home,"
    so the punchers used to say;
"And the eagles they roost in his shinin' dome
    when they happen to fly his way."
But Bill was too high for their jibes and jest,
    as serene as a summer star,
For he held the job that he liked the best,
    he was boss of the Blue Dog bar.

Once, in his early and wild career
    while riding a salty string,
He laid his twine on a longhorn steer
    and bobbled the whole dum thing.
Something happened, and when the dust had settled,
    the boys drew nigh,
And found that Bill had been sadly mussed,
    but he still retained one eye.

They hung his chaps on a harness peg
    and they hung his rope there, too,
Took him to town and shook a leg
    to see what the doc could do;
They sent for a new glass eye by mail—
    Oh, ours was a careless town!
The eye we ordered was blue and pale—
    Bill's original eye was brown.

Folks they traveled from near and far
    and all were athirst to see
The new addition to Johnson's bar—
    this double-eyed Bill McGee,
And never a stranger entered there
    but was struck with a sudden chill,
For the brown eye pivoted everywhere
    while the blue glass eye stood still.

He would talk to Johnny and look at Jake
    while he sold a drink to Jim,
And the three would buy for the simple sake
    of a good long look at him;
I've heard it said that
    Slewfoot Joe once encountered that awful stare,
And it sobered him up for a week or so,
    but that's neither here nor there.

Now Wild Jim Wicket lived down our way:
    while aspiring to win a wreath,
He mixed with a raging bronc one day
    and parted with all his teeth;
He was fetched to town and patched like new
    by Gooseberry Simes, the vet,
But the trouble was that he couldn't chew
    till he sent for another set.

Wild Jim walked up to the bar one night,
    rigged out in his brand new smile.
His teeth were shiny and tombstone white,
    you could see 'em for half a mile.
"Drinks for the crowd!" says he to Bill,
    and they went where all drinks go,
Then he raised his hand and the room was still.
    "But, pardner, I got no dough."

Grinning, he pulled his false teeth loose
    and slid 'em across the bar,
"Are these grinders good for the old corn juice?"
    Says Bill, "Well, I guess they are."
Bill was game though we thought we'd die,
    his face was that long and strange
As he screwed from its socket his new glass eye and said,
    "Mister, and here's your change."

# The Bigelow Boys

Billy and Ed and Joe were raised
    when the West was new,
Sons of the ranchman Bigelow
    and sons of their mother, too.
Billy, the eldest, turned to the call
    of the rope and brand,
And Ed, the next one, also yearned
    to be known as a first-rate hand.
But the youngest, Joe, was shy
    when his time to labor came,
So he let his brothers rope and tie
    and he took to the six-gun game.

First in a border town
    his youthful nerve was tried;
When the smoke cleared up
    his foe was down,
And the verdict was suicide.
Next in a gambling hall
    he discovered an extra ace,
And fired, point-blank
    as he made his call,
And settled the dealer's case.
So his reputation grew,
    though he never picked a fight,
And he became, in a year or two,
    the marshal of Malachite.

The brothers Bigelow,
    in charge of a bunch of steers,
Rode down that way, and they thought of Joe
    whom they hadn't seen for years.
They met in The Stope saloon
    and their boyhood days retold,
To the sound of a hurdy-gurdy tune
    and the clink of uneasy gold.
They looked on the drink when red,
    and Ed and Bill got wild;
"Let's lick the marshal," the brothers said,
    "our mother's darling child."
Together they made their play.
    'Twas a fierce and a lovely fight,
Till the marshal laid them both away
    with his notable left and right.

Bill awoke with a shuttered eye
    and Ed with a twisted jaw;
"Liquor!" said Bill with a mournful sigh,
"Yes, liquor," said Ed, "and law!"
And they stayed in the calaboose
    till the next day's sun went down,
When the marshal came and turned them loose
    and escorted them out of town.
They owned that he'd used them white,
Though their features were largely blue;
That he licked them both in a stand-up fight
    and drunk as much liquor, too.
Their farewell was sincere, but brief,
    as their callings were not akin,
Edward and William dealt in beef,
    while the marshal discouraged sin.

Slowly they rode away,
    neither sadder nor wiser men.
"Our mother's pet!" Bill heard Ed say,
    "but he was a baby, then."
Said Bill, "Yes, he's growed a lot;
    he's regular Western size.
Did you notice the handy way he's got
    of untyin' these family ties?"
"I recollect," said Ed,
    "when Joey began to creep."
"And mebby you recollect," Bill said,
    "that he rocked us both to sleep."
"But what the hell!" said Ed.
    "He stood for the whole darn' show,
Liquor, a fight, and board and bed.
    He sure is a Bigelow!"

# Old Bill

Young Sam went broke and hoofed it out of town,
When, on the mesa trail, came riding down
His partners of the range, a cowboy crew,
Rough-witted, ready-fisted, tough and true,
But bound to have their joke—and Sam was it,
And didn't like their talk a little bit.

"How, Sam? You took to walkin' for your health?
Or mebby-so you're lookin' for yore wealth,
Prospectin' like, and gazin' at the ground;
 Good-luck, old-timer—when you git it found!"

Another puncher turned as he rode by
And made a show of dealing, low and high,
But never said a word—while Sam, he cussed
And watched his outfit kicking up the dust.

Sam wished he had some dust safe in his kick.
Last night he'd spread his wages pretty thick
In town—and he'd seemed to overlook.
A gambler from The Dalles promptly took,
Even to young Sam's outfit, horse and gun,
Then Sammy quit because his dough was done.

Yet, as that cavalcade of punchers passed,
Old Bill, the foreman, and the very last
To pose as a Samaritan, came by,
A sort of evening twinkle in his eye,
Pulled up and told the youngster what he thought
About the easy way that he'd been caught:

Called him more names, with adjectives between,
Than ever had been either heard or seen
Till then—then slowly finished, "which, my son,
Was comin' to you. Now you've had yore fun,
Take this here lead-rope."
Sam he mouched across:
"I see you done that gambler for my hoss."

Bill nodded—once—and slowly rolled a smoke:
"Yes. That there Dalles gent would have his joke;
He run five aces on your Uncle Bill,
But he ain't runnin' now, he's keepin' still."

Sam gazed at Bill with wide, astonished eye;
"You plugged him!" Bill just gazed across the sky
And pulled the flop of his old Stetson hat,
"Well, son, there's some alive would call it that.
Jest fork your hoss, set straight, don't bow yore head,
Or tell the boys a gosh-durned word I said.
Come on! *Yo're* livin' yet, and you are young;
But you'll be older, next time you git stung."

Bill drew his gun—poked out an empty shell,
And Sam rode thoughtful-like, for quite a spell.

# That Was Maw

Her name was Martha Bailey,
    she was smilin', plump, and strong,
Old Jim Bailey was her husband,
    not so wide but plenty long;
They run a bunch of cattle
    rangin' south of Mormon Lake,
Maw Bailey did the cookin'—
    Oh, them apple pies and cake!

Maw would scold us, smart and sudden,
    us a-playin' of some trick,
But she'd nurse us like a angel
    if a waddie tooken sick;
She was doctor, cook, and foreman;
    on the ranch her word was law,
Old Jim Bailey called her Mrs.,
    but us punchers called her Maw.

Once the Injuns took the warpath,
    stealin' stock and killin' whites;
Maw was fussin' in the kitchen,
    puttin' cookin' things to rights;
We was out with Jim,
    a-workin , never dreamin' of a raid,
When some snaky-eyed Apaches
    tried to put Maw in the shade.

"How!" says one, pertendin' peaceful,
    but Maw Bailey knew his game,
He was packin' of a rifle
    and his face weren't painted tame.
"How?" says Maw—and then she showed him,
    swingin' high and seein' red,
As she let the skillet flicker
    and she knocked that Injun dead.

Then she grabbed Jim Bailey's shotgun
    what was standin' by the door,
And she sent another Injun
    where he'd never been before;
When she loosed the second barrel
    them there Injuns quit the show,
And we found her cryin' gentle,
    rollin' out some biscuit dough.

That was Maw. She'd scold like thunder,
    but she kept on makin' pies,
And to see a sick man suffer
    fetched the tears up in her eyes.
But you couldn't fool her nohow;
    if some hand that Jim had hired
Didn't pass her first inspection
    he got fed—but he got fired.

Once, when Jim was feelin' poorly
    and the round-up was at hand,
Maw put on her boots and Stetson,
    hired a cook, and took command,
Every outfit in the valley
    set up straight and rode polite,
With the hobbles on their cussin'
    when Maw Bailey come in sight.

When young Brady was carousin',
 drunk in Snowflake night and day,
Maw just saddled up her pony
 and she drifted down that way.
No, she didn't try to shame him,
 though her blood was on the boil,
She just drug him to the rancho
 and she fed him castor oil.

Maw took sick one ragin' winter,
 and it knocked us from our purch;
Sunday mornin', on the quiet,
 five of us rode down to church.
Jim Bailey went and told her,
 and she says to him, "Do tell!
If a shock will cure bronchitis—
 mercy sakes! I'm gettin' well."

Maw was one of them there wimmen,
 and I reckon they're the best,
That was solid, wise, and handy
 in the winnin' of the West;
"Feed your men and critters plenty,
 mend your fences, mind the law,
Keep your face and conscience shinin',
 and you'll make it!"—That was Maw.

# Mesa Magic

"Speakin' general of hoss'es,
    *in a kind of offhand way,"*—
See the mesa stealing splendor
    from the magic of the sun,
And the flowers nodding in the grass
    like children at their play,
*"That there Toby hoss of mine was lots of fun."*

*"Just how much that hoss could sabe—*
    *'course he couldn't read, but, well,"*—
While the mountain shadows mingling
    lay like pools above the sand,
As the gentle Padre climbs the stair
    to ring the mission bell,—
*"That there Toby hoss could always understand."*

*"Did you ever know a hoss to fall In love?*
    *Some funny, too,"*—
Making music o'er the silence
    of the eventide, aglow
With the Spanish girls' serapes,
    red and yellow, pink and blue,—
*"Yes, that Toby hoss he set up for a beau."*

*"He used to come and nicker soft,*
    *a-peekin' through the bars,"*—
Till the pretty colors vanish
    in the swift and starry change
Of the sky from blue to velvet-black
    and silver flame of stars,—
*"At a lady-hoss he fancied on the range."*

"He'd act pow'ful polite and bow his head—
    to get some grass,"—
Desert magic and the mystery
    of an Arizona night,
While across the brown adobes
    flitting shadows form and pass;—
"There is no use talkin', Toby was polite."

"But that lady-hoss was scornful,
    fat, and acted like a goat,"—
Dancing shadows of the pepper-tree
    by desert breeze caressed,
While the little owl awakens
    with his hushed and plaintive note,—
"But of all the hosses, Toby liked her best."

"'Twas a interestin' courtin',
    with the line-fence in between,"—
To the moonlight like a fiery mist
    upon the mesa spread,
And the world is but a bubble
    in the soft and silver sheen,—
"Say, I reckon you ain't heard a word I said."

# Under the Joshua Tree

Way out there where the sun is boss,
    Under the Joshua tree,
  'Long came a man on a played-out hoss,
    Under the Joshua tree.

Says he, "I reckon I'm a ding-dang fool
    For gettin' het up when I might stay cool:
If you are a hoss—then I'm a mule,"
    Under the Joshua Tree.

"The sink's gone dry and the trail's gone wrong,"
    Under the Joshua tree.
"I'm gettin' weak—and you ain't strong,"
    Under the Joshua tree.

"As sure as my name is Jo Bill Jones,
    We got to-quit right here," he groans,
"And the buzzards 'll git our hides and bones,"
    Under the Joshua tree.

Now that hoss wa'n't much on family pride,
 Under the Joshua tree,
But he aimed to save his ole gray hide,
 Under the Joshua tree.

He says to hisself: "The world's gone dry,
 But there's no sense quittin' while you can try,"
So he cocked one foot and he shut one eye,
 Under the Joshua tree.

Bill Jones went crawlin' round and round,
 Under the Joshua tree,
Diggin' like a dog in the bone-dry ground,
 Under the Joshua tree:

But the hoss stood still on his three feet,
 Lookin' like he was plumb dead beat,
Till he seen his chance—and he done it neat,
 Under the Joshua tree.

Ole Bill he riz right in the air,
 Under the Joshua tree,
And oh, my Gosh, how he did swear!
 Under the Joshua tree:

With a hoss-shoe branded on his pants
 He let three whoops and he done a dance,
While the ole hoss waited for another chance,
 Under the Joshua tree.

Ole Bill stood up, for he couldn't sit
 Under the Joshua tree,
And he rubbed the place where the hoss-shoe hit,
 Under the Joshua tree:

Says he: "By Gum, I'm a-seein' red!
    And I'm blink-blank sure that you ain't dead—"
And it wa'n't no cooler for what he said,
    Under the Joshua tree.

He forked that hoss like he'd never been,
    Under the Joshua tree,
His head was thick, but his jeans was thin,
    Under the Joshua tree:

He pulled out slow, but he made the ride,
    With the ole hoss thinkin' to hisseif, inside,
"I put in a kick, and I saved my hide,"
    Under the Joshua tree.

There ain't no moral to this here song,
    Under the Joshua tree,
If you don't go right you'll sure go wrong,
    Under the Joshua tree:

But settin' and lookin' at a ole hoss-shoe,
    And figurin' luck will pull you through,
Don't always work—there's hoss-sense, too,
    Under the Joshua tree.

# Ridin' to the Baile

San Antone's a Texas town:
  *Ridin' to the baile.*
Top your hoss and rein him roun',
  *Ridin' to the baile.*

Stars are shinin' big and bright,
  Mebby-so a pretty night:
And everybody's feelin' right.
  *Ridin' to the baile.*

Yonder shows the open door,
  *Ridin' to the baile.*
Seems I heard that tune before,
  *Ridin' to the baile.*

Watch 'em steppin', see 'em prance!
  Like it was their only chance:
Say, let's show 'em how to dance,
  *Ridin' to the baile.*

Put your pistol out of sight,
  *Ridin' to the baile.*
Act like you was raised polite,
  *Ridin' to the baile.*

Just a nip—and that's enough.
  Whee! But that is flamin' stuff!
'Nother nip? I call your bluff,
  *Ridin' to the baile.*

Now for steppin' off a Square.
 *Ridin' to the baile.*
What's that ruckus over there?
 *Ridin' to the baile.*

Shucks! We just got started grand,
 Now my outfit's made a stand:
'Skuse me while I take a hand,
 *Ridin' to the baile.*
. . . . . . . . . . . . . . . . . . . . . . . . . . . . .
That your husband that I sp'iled!
 *Ridin' to the baile.*
Thought you eyed me kind of wild:
 *Ridin' to the baile.*

Shoo! That ruckus wa'n't no fight!
 Our boys always is polite:
Why, they wa'n't a gun in sight!
 *Ridin' to the baile.*

Start the music—let 'er squeal!
 *Ridin' to the baile.*
Shake your leg and stomp your heel!
 *Ridin' to the baile.*

Swing your pardners! Do-se-do!
 Bend your back and bow down low;
Dance till you can't dance no mo',
 *Ridin' to the baile.*

# The Cowboys' Ball

## (With a change of tune)

*Yip! Yip! Yip! Yip! tunin' up the fiddle;*
    You an' take yo 'r pardner there, standin' by the wall!
*Say "How!" make a bow, and sashay down the middle;*
    Shake yo'r leg lively at the Cowboys' Ball.

Big feet, little feet, all the feet a-clickin';
    Everybody happy and the goose a-hangin' high;
Lope, trot, hit the spot, like a colt a-kickin';
    Keep a stompin' leather while you got one eye.

Yah! Hoo! Larry! would you watch his wings a-floppin',
    Jumpin' like a chicken that is lookin' for its head;
Hi! Yip! Never slip, and never think of stoppin',
    Just keep yo'r feet a-movin' till we all drop dead!

High heels, low heels, moccasins and slippers;
    Real ole rally 'round the dipper and the keg!
Uncle Ed's gettin' red—had too many dippers;
    Better get him hobbled or he'll break his leg!

*Yip! Yip! Yip! Yip! tunin' up the fiddle;*
    Pass him up another for his arm is gettin' slow.
*Bow down! right in town—and sashay down the middle;*
    Got to keep a-movin' for to see the show!

Yes, mam! Warm, mam? Want to rest a minute?
    Like to get a breath of air lookin' at the stars?
All right! Fine night—dance? There's nothin' in it!
    That's my pony there, peekin' through the bars.

Bronc, mam? No, mam! Gentle as a kitten!
    Here, boy! Shake a hand! Now, mam, you can see;
Night's cool. What a fool to dance, instead of sittin'
    Like a gent and lady, same as you and me.

*Yip! Yip! Yip! Yip! tunin' up the fiddle;*
    Well, them as likes the exercise sure can have it all!
*Right wing, lady swing, and sashay down the middle . . .*
    But this beats dancin' at the Cowboys' Ball.

# Pony Tracks

I was ridin' for the Blue,
    When she wrote to me from France;
Wrote and sent her picture, too!
    Talk about that there "Romance"!

Wrote to me, the Ridin' Kid,
    Just a cattle-chain' cuss,
But you bet I'm glad she did
    Say that she had heard of us

Cowboys of the Western range;
    Kinda thought that joke the best,
For we'd call it mighty strange
    If the ranges weren't out West.

Sent her picture, and it's great!
    Slim and neat from heel to head,
Stylish dressed and settin' straight
    On a dandy thoroughbred.

Said she'd read some poetry
    All about a Roan Cayuse;
Well, I own it's up to me,
    I ain't makin' no excuse,

But sometimes I got to sing,
    When my pony jogs along;
Seems his hoofs they click and ring
    Till they've hammered out a song

Kinda like the sound of rain,
  Kinda like the sun and sky,
Shadows streakin' crost the plain,
  Little clouds a-floatin' by,

And a puncher and his hoss
  Ridin' trails that never end. . .
Well, I showed it to the boss,
  And he sent it to a friend.

Friend he owned a printin'-shop,
  And a high-tone magazine;
Say, my heart sure took a flop,
  When that poetry I seen.

Boys they joshed me stout and strong;
  Called me "Little Warblin' Kid!"
Me! I'm only six feet long
  From my boot-heels to my lid.

Wonder if her eyes are brown?
  Wonder if they're blue or gray?
Wonder if she lives in town?
  Wonder if *she'd* ever say,

"Howdy, partner!" Shucks! but she
  Never seen a Stetson hat,
Never seen a guy like me;
  And she'd never talk like that.

But I learned to say her name;
  Ask the schoolmarm straight, one day;
Print and sound ain't just the same,
  But it spells like this—"Edmée."

Wrote that she would like to ride
    Where the world is big and free,
But she says her family's pride
    Keeps her where she ought to be.

Says she's longin' for the life
    Out here where the cattle roam;
Well, I never had a wife,
    Never hung my hat to home.

Guess that letter got me hard;
    Prettiest girl I ever seen;
That 's what comes of singin', pard.
    And a high-tone magazine.

When I'm ridin' round the herd,
    And the stars are shinin' bright,
I keep practicin' that word,
    And I aim to get it right;

"Edmée." But my pony's feet,
    Keep a-arguin' and say,
Slow and steady—and repeat—
    "France is—mighty—far—away!"

# Mournful Joe

One mornin' early when the ground was froze,
Old Mournful Joe from his tarp arose,
He et his chuck, give his plate a toss,
And picked up his lariat to ketch a hoss:

Says he, "I know that I'll sure git throwed."
Him thinkin' that way, why, the bronc he knowed,
For he humped his back, give a warnin' squeal,
And left Joe tangled in a wagon-wheel.

*It's Hi Yi Yippy and a Too La Lay,*
*You'll sure git scattered if you feel that way!*

Once Joe was sittin' in the line-shack door,
When a cyclone started for to rip and roar,
And instead of crawlin' to a deep coulee,
That darned old waddie clumb a pinon tree:

Says he, "I know what I'm goin' to git,"
And he hung to the branches as the cyclone hit,
It tore his whiskers and it sprained his back,
But it never touched a button on the old line-shack.

*It's Hi Yi Yippy and a Too La Lay,*
*You'll sure git scattered if you feel that way!*

Joe got to foolin' with a pick and drill,
Muckin' and minin' on Red Rock Hill;
The sun was shinin' and the air was hot,
And he was a-sweatin' when he tamped the shot:

Says he, "I'm bettin' of my Sunday shoes,
That somethin'll happen when I light this fuse:"
And I reckon the birds weren't much surprised,
When he come up flyin' like he advertised.

*It's Hi Yi Yippy and a Too La Lay,*
*You'll sure git scattered if you feel that way!*

He was always mournin', but a-doin' fine,
And he kept on livin' up to ninety-nine,
He'd done quit minin' and a-chasin' steers,
So we figured he'd make it to a hundred years.

Says he, "I'm bettin' on no such thing,
Somethin'll happen and the bell will ring:"
Come half-past-eleven he begins to snore,
And at twelve he was sleepin' on the Golden Shore.

*It's Hi Yi Yippy and a Too La Lay,*
*You'll sure git scattered if you feel that way!*

# The Old-Timer

Morning on the Malibu,
    mist across the ranges;
Ponies bucking everywhere.
    "Whoop! and let'er buck!
Bud is standin' on his head;
    Bill is makin' changes
In his style of cussin'
    and he's havin' plenty luck."

"When it comes to ridin' broncs—
    listen to me, stranger—
Takes a hoss what is a hoss
    to pile your Uncle Jim;
Whoa! You think you're goin' to dump
    a ole-time Texas Ranger?
Just excuse me for a spell;
    I'll take it out of *him*.

"Hump, you side of bacon, you!
    Spin till you git dizzy!
I could roll a cigarette
    while you are doin' such.
Mebby now you think
    that you are keepin' me right busy?
Wish't I had my knittin',
    for you don't amount to much.

"As I was sayin', stranger—
    Whump! Now, ding that pinto devil!
Gosh-and-what-goes-with-it,
    but he piled me sure enough;
I was ridin' on the square
    and now I'm on the level;
Serves me right for talkin'
    and pertendin' I was tough.

*"Ought to buy a rockin' chair!*
  *Git a pair of crutches!*
Hear the boys a joshin' me now
    they got the chance;
*Baldy 's diggin' angle-worms with his nose!*
    Now such is
Mighty childish joshin' . . .
    Say, 'fore you was wearin' pants

"I was ridin' broncs
    and didn't have to pull no leather;
Broncs that pawed a star down
    every time they took a jump.
And I wern't sixty-two them days;
    I didn't feel the weather;
Give me forty year off
    and I'll lick you in a lump!

"Laugh, you movin'-picture kids;
    think *you're* punchin' cattle?
I was raised in Texas
    where a steer is called a steer;
I have done some ridin'
    that would make your eye-teeth rattle;
From the Tonto to Montana,
    ridin' range for forty year.

"Guess I got 'em thinkin' now—
    thinkin' strong and quiet,
Mad at *them?* Why, stranger,
    I'm a ole-time buckaroo,
Don't git mad at nothin'. . .
    If they're livin' let 'em try it,
Ridin' range and ropin'
    when they're turned of sixty-two."

# I Knew a Boy

I knew a boy who, at the pasture gate,
    Shouted and laughed to see the ponies run;
A barefoot urchin, sturdy, live, elate,
    Who rode them all—the worst and best—for fun.

Was tumbled from the worst; stuck to the best
    And loved them; yea! nor deemed the old rail fence
A barrier to dismount for, but made test;
    Aptly the soul of "Whither going hence?"

Knew not nor cared no more than did his steed,
    Unbitted, playful-wild, and ne'er in hand,
Till, breathless, in the pasture mullein-weed
    They stopped; the "Whoa!" gratuitous command.

I knew a boy—perchance it was the same,
    Though time had wrought its certain outward change—
Who still though seldom silent—played the game
    With branding-iron and rope on Western range.

The clean, clear tan of sun upon his cheek,
    The light of morning in his laughing eye;
Seeking adventure to the farthest peak,
    Or watching dream-led cavalcades go by.

Swiftly the golden shuttle of the dream
    Darted across the loom of sunlit hours,
Till romance, tiring of the weaver's beam,
    Vanished among the nodding prairie-flowers.

The high trail dwindled in the sunset glow,
    And laughter ceased; instead came Reverie
To pace beside him, silent, wan, and slow,
    Until his wondering eyes beheld the sea.

Sadly he watched the gray gulls dip and ride
    The swollen ridges rushing to the shore,
Then rise to wing across the sounding tide
    That drummed a slow, reiterant "Nevermore."

Then something, that had slept throughout the years
    Deep in his heart, awakened: "Nay! my joy
Shall not be tarnished by these futile tears,
    Because"—he laughed—"because. . . I knew a boy. . . ."

# Trail-to-Glory

Could old Trail-to-Glory preach!
   Seems he understood this land
   Where you have to learn first-hand
      (Without books and such, to teach)
   One brand from another brand.

     Having nothing much to lose,
   When a Sunday come around,
   We would squat here on the ground,
     Twenty of us buckaroos,
   Never making 'ary sound

     While he opened up the ball,
   Singing first, then praying low,
   Like them little winds that blow
     Sand around the chaparral
   Kind of easy-like and slow.

     Seemed to us just like a game;
   You play this and I'll play that;
   Trail-to-Glory standing pat;
     Never working any frame,
   Never passing round the hat:

     For he warn't out for money, pard,
   Had his job, just like the rest,
   Riding, roping with the best,
     Working hard and sweating hard,
   Waiting for that Day of Rest.

When it come *he* changed his clothes;
Seemed to us just like a game,
Staking all on just a Name;
    Talking quiet-like to those
That he knew he couldn't tame,
    Till, one day, the show-down came.

    Swung my rope and lass'ed a steer;
Hoss he bucked and I got piled.
Steer come at me frothing wild;
    Trail-to-Glory, riding near,
Jumped and saved me, and he smiled.

    That was all I knew a spell . . . .
Then I saw the boys around
Something stretched out on the ground;
    'T want no steer, I knew right well;
Boys a-making nary sound—
    Yes; that's all there is to tell.

# He'll Make a Hand

He joined our outfit on the drive,
  came driftin' in alone,
A kid, wolf-hungry, half-alive,
  and mostly skin and bone,
With nothin' but a played-out hoss
  that he could call his own.

Too young to be a down-and-out,
  a-ramblin' 'round the land,
His stock-in-trade some language stout,
  a smile, and plenty sand.
But Mose, the foreman, took him on and said,
  "He'll make a hand."

We combed our beds for boots and hat
  and gave what we could spare,
Mose put him on a pony
  that could take him anywhere.
And when we pushed 'em up the trail,
  you bet the Kid was there.

He weren't no angel,
  and we threw some language at the Kid;
But cussed for what he didn't do
  and cussed for what he did,
He didn't bow his neck and pitch,
  but kep' his temper hid.

The night was sultry, hot and queer,
    the clouds were movin' slow,
The Kid night-hawkin'—
    we could hear his whistlin' soft and low,
When, far away, like whisperin'
    the wind began to blow.

A shufflin' in the beddin'-ground,
    and yonder, down the hill,
A streak of white, a rumblin' sound,
    then everything was still,
When, smellin' thunder in the air,
    the herd began to mill.

Old Mose was pullin' on his boots,
    a-settin' on his bed;
"She's loadin' fast and when she shoots—"
    and that was all he said,
For something busted in the sky,
    and lit the world with red.

A spatterin' rain, a rush, a roar,
    and hell had opened wide,
The cattle down the valley floor,
    a-humpin' hoof and hide,
As right and left we swung and rode
    like blind-drunk Injuns ride.

The wind fair tore your breath away,
    the rain beat swift and cold,
The lightnin' flooded white as day,
    the thunder ripped and rolled,
And every blunderin' jump
    a chance you wouldn't grow too old.

The mornin' air come sparklin' bright,
    the hills seemed close around,
And what had happened in the night
    was hoof-marked on the ground:
Old Mose he called me to a draw
    and showed me what he found.

The Kid had done the best he could
    to head that wild stampede,
Had done like any real hand would—
    the sign was plain to read—
Not ridin' wide to swing the bunch,
    but cuttin' in the lead.

We dug a grave and covered him
    with rock and brush and sand,
And Mose he said a kind of prayer
    which all could understand:
"Old Master, give the Kid a chance.
    Down here he made a hand."

# Where the Ponies Come to Drink

Up in Northern Arizona
    there's a Ranger-trail that passes
Through a mesa, like a faëry lake
    with pines upon its brink,
And across the trail a stream runs
    all but hidden in the grasses,
Till it finds an emerald hollow
    where the ponies come to drink.

Out they fling across the mesa,
    wind-blown manes and forelocks dancing,
—Blacks and sorrels, bays and pintos,
    wild as eagles, eyes agleam;
From their hoofs the silver flashes,
    burning beads and arrows glancing
Through the bunch-grass and the gramma,
    as they cross the little stream.

Down they swing as if pretending,
    in their orderly disorder,
That they stopped to hold a pow-wow,
    just to rally for the charge
That will take them, close to sunset,
    twenty miles across the border;
Then the leader sniffs and drinks
    with fore feet planted on the marge.

One by one each head is lowered,
     till some yearling nips another,
And the playful interruption
     starts an eddy in the band:
Snorting, squealing, plunging, wheeling,
     round they circle in a smother
Of the muddy spray, nor pause
     until they find the firmer land.

My old cow-horse, he runs with 'em:
     turned him loose for good last season;
Eighteen years' hard work, his record,
     and he's earned his little rest;
And he's taking it by playing,
     acting proud, and with good reason;
Though he's starched a little forward,
     he can fan it with the best.

Once I called him—almost caught him,
     when he heard my spur-chains jingle;
Then he eyed me some reproachful,
     as if making up his mind:
Seemed to say, "Well, if I have to—
     but you know I'm living single. . . ."
So I laughed.
     In just a minute he was pretty hard to find.

Some folks wouldn't understand it,—
     writing lines about a pony,—
For a cow-horse is a cow-horse,—
     nothing else, most people think,—
But for eighteen years your partner,
     wise and faithful, such a crony
Seems worth watching for, a spell,
     down where the ponies come to drink.

# Song of the Gray Stallion

My dame was a mustang white and proud,
My sire was as black as a thunder-cloud;
I was foaled on the mesas cold and high.
Where the strong ones live and the weak ones die,
And the mountain-lion steals:

Hid in the brush I knew no fear,
With a milk-white mustang grazing near;
When the grass grew green in the summer sun,
I learned to dodge and I learned to run,
And I learned to use my heels.

Sleek and strong and a stallion grown,
I took no pace that was not my own;
I fought for life in the winter storm,
And I fought for pride when the sun grew warm,
And the mares ran, calling shrill;

Then hot with the pride of my young desire,
I drove from the band my fighting sire;
My flanks dripped red but my crest was high,
For the young must live and the old must die,
Over hollow land and hill:

So if you think to down my pride,
Build a swift loop, cowboy, build it wide,
For I 'm hard to catch and hard to tame,
I bear no brand, but I've earned my name,
The wild horse, stallion gray.

The mesa wind blows high and free,
But no wind that blows can outrun me;
You can sink your rowels out of sight,
And quirt your horse till his eye rolls white,
But I'll be far away.

# Outlaw

A day we followed the wild horse herd,
    A day and another day;
A fresh mount and a quick word,
    At the relay.

Varney's horse turned a hoolihan,
    Varney quit.
A good hand. But a dead man
    Is out of it.

Buck and I followed the wild horse herd,
    The last day;
A fresh mount and the same word
    At the relay:
"The Black Storm leads them yet!"

Gray rock, gray sky and the trail gray,
    The cold stars gone.
Crowded, the wild mares surged away,
    Breasting the dawn.

Their hoofs on the granite rumbled.
    At the cañon ledge
A yearling nickered, stumbled,
    Went over the edge.

The herd strung out to follow
    Down the old track;
But the stallion shied from the hollow
    And broke back.

The rim of the sun spread fire,
    Down the far height,
Flamed round the storm-black sire,
    A glory of light.

A second—it seemed an age;
    Up the sun rolled.
The stallion reared in his rage,
    His hoofs raw gold.

Ears flat, crest curved,
    A snake's eye,
He charged, reared again, swerved,
    Hammered the sky.

Buck flipped a loop, took a dally;
    The rope steamed.
I heeled him. Blind mad in a rally.
    He battled and screamed.

Fight! Just whisper we fought him
    Yes, all the way!
Savage and sullen we brought him,
    To the relay.

Three ropes on him we eared him,
    In the log corral.
The boys on the top rail cheered him,
    As he dealt us hell.

He wasted each man that would ride him.
    Buck was first;
And the seventh and last that tried him
    He crippled the worst.

The night fire warm on our faces,
    The wind down,
We talked of people and places,
    Of range and town.

Quick hoofs drummed out our talking,
    Then, a cool surprise,
As Buck from the shadows stalking
    Answered our eyes:

"Too wicked to keep, too noble to kill,
    And so,
I turned him loose. He's over the hill,
    I let him go."

Down the sky shot a star,
    As a rocket flares.
Black Storm, ranging far,
    Called to his mares.

# The Round Corral

Buck Yardlaw in the round corral
    leaned hard against the rope,
His rigid muscles bunched
    from hip to straining shoulder-slope:
Alone he fought the outlaw horse—
    a lusty, dusty fight;
Threw him and forced the blind
    across red eyeballs ringed with white.

Then let him up and saddled him,
    caught cinch upon the swing,
And cautious-swift the latigo
    slipped binding through the ring:
Set close the choking hackamore,
    drew knot and loop to place,
Stepped back and wiped the running sweat
    from off his weathered face:

Swung to the saddle, flicked the blind:
    then lunge and plunge and rear,
While rope and rowel strove to break
    blind hate gone mad with fear:
Rope slashed and reddened rowel stung:
    the outlaw squealed and fell,
And Yardlaw lay, a huddled shape, still,
    in the round corral.

The morning sun shone on the sage—
  wide miles of dusty gray;
Shone shimmering on the round corral—
  on Yardlaw where he lay;
Shone down upon the outlaw horse,
  red-trembling as he stood
A mockery of conquering man's wild pride
  and hardihood.

Buck Yardlaw raised upon his arm
  and shaped his mouth to curse
The stirrup where his foot had hung,
  the sun-swept universe,
The outlaw, and the round corral—
  when spake a gentle Voice,
While, listening, Yardlaw grinned his pain,
  nor had he other choice.

"Who rules with love of man for beast
  need never rule with steel.
Beyond the need of conquering
  ye ply the roweled heel:
Red-raw ye plough the quivering flesh,
  or ring the tender jaw:
Subdue or kill!
  Nor would ye teach the brute a higher law."

"And I be down," Buck Yardlaw said,
  "yet I will stand again,
And break the bronco to my use
  or hide myself from men,
There is no law that I've heard tell
  to use a bronco mild,
But I'll play square if he plays square,
  or wild if he plays wild."

"Who rules with love of man for beast . . ."
    So had the Voice begun:
Buck Yardlaw wakened to the world,
    the sagebrush in the sun;
His body was a rack of pain,
    his face was set and white;
"We'll try that higher Law," he said;
    "perhaps the Voice was right!"

Then slowly to the horse he came
    and slowly raised his hand,
Stopped as the outlaw flinched,
    but stood as gentle horses stand,
While Yardlaw loosed the slackened cinch,
    lifted the saddle clear,
Watching the fixed and burning eye,
    the undecided ear.

Each knew the other's fighting pride,
    unconquered to the end;
Yet often does the bitter foe
    become the staunchest friend.
"Of all the broncs I've ever fought,
    I reckon you're the best,"
And Yardlaw laid a fearless hand
    upon a fearless crest.

# That Roan Cayuse

Colt she was when I spied her,
    stray on the open range;
Starvin' poor, for the feed was thin
    and water-holes far between.
I roped her and threw and tied her,
    for I saw she was actin' strange;
And on her breast was a barb-wire cut—
    the worst I have ever seen.

Talk about nursin'!
    Maybe that hoss wasn't raised by hand!
Boys they joshed when they saddled up
    and when they rode in at night;
"S-s-s-h! Don't you wake the baby!
    Say, can't you understand—
Cussin' don't go in this horsepital,
    or Doc'll get mad and bite!"

Look at her now! Like copper,
    shinin' and sleek and strong!
Follow a mountain trail all day
    and finish a-steppin' high.
Nothin' out here can stop her,
    and she lopes like a swallow's song.
Wicked as fire to a stranger—
    but as gentle to me as pie.

Look at her straight-up ears,
   now, listenin' to you and me!
Her eyes are askin' questions;
   wonderin' what's to do.
Understands what she hears?
   Now, watch when I call and see
How she'll circle around to my side
   and flatten her ears at you.

Bronco? Don't pay to quirt her.
   I'm bronco myself, some days,
Pitchin' when luck is a-ridin' me hard
   and pilin' it if I can.
But a quick, hard word will hurt her—
   for a hoss has peculiar ways;
Use any hoss like a human
   and he'll treat you just like a man.

You'd ride her? That's not surprisin'
   for judgin' your legs, you could.
But flowers are scarce at this time of year
   and there isn't a parson nigh.
She sure needs exercisin';
   't would do her a lot of good,
But I'd hate to see you a-flyin',
   'cause you ain't built right to fly.

Remember that old-time sayin',
   cinched up in a two-bit rhyme?
"There isn't a hoss that can't be rode."
   And many a rider tries,
But when it comes to stayin',
   why, you can't stay every time;
"There isn't a man that can't be throwed"
   is the place where the song gets wise.

"That roan cayuse of the Concho":
    when a hoss has a name like that,
You can figure its reputation
    without askin' another word.
You can roll it up in your poncho,
    or bury it under your hat,
It's just like that picture-writin'—
    means lots that you haven't heard.

You straighten them ears up pronto!
    You, showin' your teeth at me!
Here, now, you quit your bitin'—
    do you think I'm a bale of hay?
You'd buy her? She heard you say it—
    ears flat and eye rollin', see!
Well, she is the lady to talk to—
    and I guess that's your answer, eh?

## Little Bronc

Little Bronc, I'm goin' to ride you—
    you a-hidin' in between
        Blue and Baldy! Think you're bluffin'
        With your snortin' and your puffin';
        Quit! And save yourself a roughin',
Guess you sabe what I mean.

Yes, my loop is wide and trailin'—
    and your eye a-showin' white:
        Reckon that I got to show you,
        For I broke you and I know you,
        Mebby-so I got to throw you
'Fore I get them cinches tight.

'Tain't no use! I got you comin'
    and I aim to take a chance:
        Pitch and squeal and fight ag'in' it!
        I'll be with you, in a minute;
        Hell to breakfast—all that's in it,
I'm your pardner for this dance!

Grunt you! Forty pounds of saddle—
    and you swellin' like a cow:
        I was raised down on the Tonto,
        Where they break and ride 'em pronto:
        You're fork-lightnin' to git onto,
But I aim to fork you, now.

Whee! Now just unwind your feelin's!
  Get them wrinkles from your hide!
    Here's the iron for your balkin',
    Just stiff-mad because I'm talkin',
    And you aim to set me walkin',
Well, you bronc—I aim to ride!

Steady! Thought you knowed the iron!
  Guess your pitchin' fit is done.
    Now dig in and scatter dirt, you!
    Shakin' 'cause you think I'll quirt you?
    Shucks! I never aimed to hurt you,
I'm just playin' with you, son!

See that spot of green, down yonder?
  That's the town of San Jose.

    Thirty mile we come a-sweatin',
    Tail a-switchin', ears a-frettin',
    But your boss is still a-settin'
In the hull, and goin' to stay.

Howdy, John! What, sell this pony?
  Say, you're talkin' through your hat;
    This here bronc is wise to ropin',
    Thirty miles we come, a-lopin',
    Gentle? Sure! And—well, here's hopin'!
Yes, I'll take a hundred, flat.

Sold that pitchin' chunk of trouble,
  and there ain't no use to stay.
    Air 'll be thick here, after dinner,
    When John forks that outlaw sinner:
    And I'm goin' where it's thinner:
Yes, I'm leavin' San Jose.

# The Bronco

The bronco's mighty wild and tough,
    And full of outdoor feelin's:
His feet are quick, his ways are rough,
    He's careless in his dealin's.

Each mornin' he must have his spree,
    And hand you plenty trouble
A-pitchin' round the scenery
    Till you are seein' double.

Or mebby-so, you think he's broke,
    And do a little braggin';
"Plumb gentle hoss!" he sees the joke,
    And leaves—with reins a-draggin'.

Or, mebby-so, you think he'll jump
    That little three-foot railin':
When all he does is stop and hump,
    And stay—while you go sailin'.

But when his pitchin' fit is done,
    And ropin', cuttin', brandin',
Is on the bill—I'll tell you, son,
    He works with understandin'.

At workin' stock he's got his pride:
    Dust rollin', boys a-yellin'—
He'll turn your steer, and make you ride,
    And he don't need no tellin'.

Perbaps you're standin' middle-guard,
    Or ridin' slow, night-hawkin':
And then your bronc is sure your pard,
    At loafin', or at walkin'.

Or, when the lightnin' flashes raw,
    And starts the herd a-flyin',
He's off to head 'em down the draw,
    Or break your neck, a-tryin'.

A bronc, he sure will take his part,
    At gettin' there, or stayin':
He'll work until be breaks his heart,
    But he don't sabe playin'.

He may be wild, he may be tough,
    And full of outdoor feelin's:
But he's all leather, sure enough,
    And he puts through his dealin's.

# Largo

Bought him off the Navajos—shadow of a pony,
    Over near the Largo draw, runnin' up and down;
Twenty pesos turned the trick—broke me cold and stony;
    Then I set to figure as I rambled into town.

'Fore I had the feel of him, twice he like to throwed me;
    He didn't have to figure sums, cause he wasn't broke;
Then he took to runnin' and unknown'-like, he showed me
    Speed that was surprisin' in a twenty-dollar joke.

Wiry little Navajo, no bigger than a minute;
    Did a heap of restin' up when he got the chance,
But. . . ever stop a pin-wheel just to locate what was in it.
    Findin' unexpected you was sittin' on your pants?

That was him—the Largo hoss; didn't take to schoolin';
    Relayed out of Calient' into Santa Fe;
Fifty mile of kickin' sand and not a wink of foolin'
    When he hit the desert trail windin' down that way.

Once they put a blooded hoss on the trail behind him;
    Passed me like a Kansas blow; Largo didn't mind,
Kept a-runnin', strong and sweet. Reckoned that we'd find him
    Like we did, in twenty mile, busted, broke, and blind.

Ever see a Injun race? Times I could 'a' sold him
    For a dozen cattle—a most interestin' price;
Set to figurin' ag'in—bought the mare that foaled him.
    Shucks! Her colts they couldn't beat a herd of hobbled mice.

Took the brush and curry-comb—thought he'd understand it. . .
    Him a-loafin' lazy with his nose across the bars;
Reckon dudes comes natural; as hard as he could land it,
    He druv home his opinion while I gathered up the stars.

That was him—the Largo hoss; never saw another
    Desert hoss could beat him when he started out to float.
Pedigree? He hadn't none; a pony was his mother,
    And judgin' from his looks I guess his father was a goat.

That's him now a-standin' there, sleepy—like and dreamin';
    Sell him? Thought you'd ask me that. Northern mail is late
Just three hours. No, not to-day, pardner. Without seemin'
    Brash—from here to Santa Fe we'll wipe it off the slate.

Bought him off the Navajos—broke me cold and stony;
    But I got a roll to-day—tell you what I'll do—Ridin' South?
Well, pardner, I'll just give you that there pony,
    If we ain't in Santa Fe three hours ahead of you.

# Burro

Beloved burro the ample ear,
   Philosopher, gray hobo of the dunes,
Delight of children, thistle-chewing seer,
   From Lebanon and old, how many moons?

Muse of Manana: sturdy foe of haste;
   True to yourself in every attitude;
A statue of dejection, shaggy-faced,
   Or plodding with your pack of cedar-wood;

Stopping to turn about, with motion stiff,
   As though you half imagined something wrong:
Wondering if you were there complete, or if
   The other half forgot to come along.

What melancholy thoughts bestir your heart
   When, like an ancient pump, you lift a tone,
Lose it and lift another—with an art
   Bequeathed to none on earth, save you alone?

Your melody means something deep, unseen;
 Desert contralto you are called: perchance
An ear attuned to mysteries might glean
 More from your song than simple assonance.

You sing the truth, without a touch of guile:
 And truth were sad enough—yet your fond guise
Of bland sincerity provokes a smile,
 And so the world is richer—burro-wise.

Thus do you serve twofold, in that you please
 That subtle sense that loves the ludicrous
Nor scorns affection. Oh, Demosthenes
 Of Andalusia, left to preach to us!

Dogging the shadows of some empty street,
 Content with what your indolence may find,
You let the world roll on, and keep your feet,
 Or let it run, and still you stray behind.

# Chance

Sixty miles from a homestead,
    straight as the crow can fly,
We camped in the Deadwood foothills.
    Mineral? Yes—and gold.
Three of us in the outfit;
    the burro and Chance and I;
Chance wasn't more than a pup then',
    goin' on two years old.

Already he knew the music
    that a desert rattler makes
When, glimmerin' under a yucca,
    he'd seen 'em coil to spring;
But he didn't need no teachin'
    to keep him away from snakes;
You should seen his tail go under
    when he heard a rattler sing!

Town-folks called him the "Killer,"
    and I reckon that they was right;
Deep in the chest, wolf-muscled,
    and quicker than fire in tow;
But one of the kind that never
    went out of his way to fight,
Though he'd tackle a corral of wild-cats
    if I gave him the word to go.

There was more to him than his fightin'—
    he was wise; it was right good fun
To see him usin' his head-piece
    when the sun was a-fryin' eggs,
Trailin' along with the outfit
    and cheatin' the desert sun
By keepin' into the shadow
    right close to my burro's legs.

I knew that some day I'd lose him,
    for the desert she don't wait long;—
Hosses and dogs and humans,
    none of 'em get too old;
Gold? Looks good in a story
    and sounds right good in a song,
But the men that go out and get it—
    they know what they pay for gold!

If I struck a ledge that showed me a million,—
    the whole thing mine,—
I'd turn it over to-morrow
    (and never so much as glance
At the papers the law-sharks frame up
    and hand you a pen to sign)
For a look at my old side-pardner,
    the "Killer," that I called, "Chance."

Why? Well, my eyes, one mornin',
    was blinkin' to shake a dream,
And Chance was sleepin' beside me,
    breathin' it long and deep.
When I saw a awful somethin'
    and I felt I was like to scream. . . .
There was a big, brown rattler
    coiled in my arm, asleep.

Move . . . and I knew he'd get me.
    Waitin', I held my breath,
Feelin' the sun get warmer,
    wonderin' what to do,
Tryin, to keep my eyes off
    that shinin' and sudden death,
When Chance he lifted his head up
    and slow come the rattler, too.

"Take him!" I tried to whisper.
    Mebby I did. I know
Chance's neck was a-bristle
    and his eyes on the coiled-up snake;
Its head was a-movin' gentle—
    like weeds when the south winds blow
When Chance jumped in. . .the "Killer,". . .
    Do that for a pardner's sake?

I'd like to think that I'd do it . . .
    Up there in the far-off blue
Old Marster He sits a-jedgin'
    such things. Can you tell me why,
Knowin' what he had comin',
    he went at it fightin'—true;
Tore that snake into ribbons,
    then crawled to the brush to die?

Never come near me after;
    knew that he'd got his call;
How come I went and shot him.
    God I can see his eyes!
See where those pointed shadows
    run down that canyon wall?
That there's his tombstone, stranger,
    bigger than money buys.

# Song of the Mule

Sing if ye will, of the thoroughbred,
    and the fine old Morgan breed,
The Arab sire with his noble head
    and his gift of grace and speed,
Of cavalry mount and range cayuse—
    yea, follow the old-time rule;
But here is the song of a stouter muse—
    the song of the homely mule!

Unsung pedestrian Pegasus,
    child of the True Romance,
A worthy theme for the best of us
    in the study of assonance;
A royal gift when the Spanish Don
    held half of the world in fee;
Banners fade—yet the mule goes on,
    in spite of his pedigree.

Sorrel or chestnut, brown or black,
    fleabitten gray or roan,
Zebra stripe on his legs or back,
    a lineage all his own;
His hide is tough, his voice is loud,
    his frame is uncouth and strong;
He shows no pride as a horse is proud—
    but he knows where his feet belong.

He came with the outpost ambulance,
    he followed the new frontier,
He was more than a long-eared circumstance
    as a railroad pioneer;
He blazed the way for the iron trail
    and carried the scant supplies,
Or toiled at grading and tucked his tail
    and hee-hawed to the skies.

When scouts ride into the borderland,
    the mule is first to go,
The chosen mount of a wary band
    who trail an elusive foe;
Hunger and heat and thirst pursue,
    cinches and belts grow slack,—
Guide and horse may make it through—
    but ever the mule comes back.

Yea, smile at his awkward fashioning,
    mock at his weird refrain,
But watch him work in a freighter's string,
    and watch him jump the chain
On a mountain grade, with a load of ore,
    when the brake-shoes grind and jerk—
And a half-mile drop to the Golden Shore
    if he doesn't observe his work!

In outland venture, in mine or mart,
    he's the handiest tool alive,
Show him his work—he takes his part
    and strives as the builders strive;
Rusty, dusty, rugged, and slow,
    he ambles from sun to sun,
Trails a trace to the barn—and lo!
    The thing that was dreamed is done.

Hut! you Jerry! Hych! Jake!
    The dump-carts jolt and groan,
The slithering fresno rounds the stake,
    the crushers vomit stone;
Dust, machinery, mules, and men,
    whistle and tramway gong,
Over the world and back again—
    this is your glory-song!

# The Mule-Skinner

The clack and clatter of the chain;
    the staggering pull to top the crest,
The break-line slack; below,
    the plain and twenty mules, in pairs, abreast.

The heated tires that grind and smoke;
    the nimble leaders swinging wide;
The swirls of powdered dust that choke,
    and curl along the mountain side.

Careless of poise and keen of eye
    the skinner on the wheeler's back
Condemns his mules expressively—
    and takes a little jerk-line slack.

"Roll on, old wagon, we're going home!
    Hump, you buck-skins, hop-it-along!
Jump, you Jerry-old-Jereboam. Listen—
    I'll sing you a little song:

    "Oh, I had a girl in San Antone,
        She had a beau lived down that way. . . .
    I met up with him one night alone. . . .
        That's why I'm skinnin' mules to-day.

    "Oh, there was a hoss in San Antone;
        I borrowed that hoss and I come away,
    Fanning it fast on that white-faced roan. . . .
        That's why I'm skinnin' mules to-day."

The blind wheel worries in the rut;
    the slow sand follows up the tire;
The distance shows a herder's hut
    below the ridge in sunset fire,

As o'er the grim wheel-gutted plain,
    silent beneath its weight of years,
The mules plod on with grunt and strain,
    with nodding heads and swinging ears;

A cowboy turns and waves his hand.
    Then, with the twinkle of his spur,
Rides slowly toward the foothill land,
    a lone and proud adventurer;

But reins and listens, nods and smiles
    with head aslant, as low and long
Across the hushed and stagnant miles
    he hears the echo of a song:

    "I ain't going back to San Antone;
        Haven't time to go down that way,
    For I got a girl and a kid of my own. . . .
        That's why I'm skinnin' mules to-day. . . .

    "Skinning mules on the old Tejon,
        And believe me, sister, it ain't no play;
    But I got a girl and a kid of my own,
        That's why I'm skinnin' mules to-day."

# The Pack Train

Oh, some prefer the beaten track
  from city unto city,
    With fence and fence on either side
      and smoke at either end,
Nor know the joy of trail and pack—
  and silence—mores the pity:
    It's *hurry! hurry!* everywhere,
      and little time to spend.

The morning's on the hills of blue
  with mist across them blowing:
    Then hang and balance each kyack
      the dead-weight of the other,
And lay the diamond neat and true,
  for up the range we're going;
    Heave hard and steal an inch of slack,
      and if you can, another.

All trim and stout? Then string 'em out
and start 'em slow and steady:
Our trail is up the hills of blue
with sun on ridge and hollow:
The leader knows what he's about—
he's wise, but never heady,
So now there's nothing else to do
but fork your horse and follow.

Around the bend, along the ledge—
the clouds are rolling under,
From shore to shore like drifted snow,
and in the distance gleaming,
A thread of gold, the ocean-edge:
we're higher than the thunder;
With blue above and gray below,
and in between we're dreaming.

It's creak of rope and plod of hoof—
a sort of outland rhyming,
As up the grade to timber-line
we make it mile by mile,
We're riding on the morning's roof—
it took a bit of climbing
To top the land of spruce and pine—
so let 'em rest awhile.

Then down along this rocky ridge
dividing all creation,
The backbone of a giant ram
that humps to meet the sky,
A narrow but a solid bridge
to reach the Ranger Station,
And there's the flag
where Uncle Sam is watching, far an high.

It's closer to the stars than most.
  Well, all the packs are riding:
    It's fuss and fiddle down the grade
     and shuffle through the Pass,
And 'way out yonder is the coast
  the morning mists were hiding,
    And here's the camp,
     with plenty shade and mountain meadow grass.

So slack the ropes and drop the packs
  and let 'em go to grazing,
    They've earned a rest—
     they put it through two hours ahead of night:
Just watch 'em roll to dry their backs:
  they won't need any hazing
    To feed and water on The Blue—
     and how's *your* appetite?

# The Sheep

An undulating, dusty patch, they move
  Along the margin of the cañon stream.

Beside the herder stand the watchful dogs,
With ears alert and eyes that read his face.

He sees his semblance by the midday sun
Dwarfed on the glaring sand.

                    The sheep move on
And vanish in the slumberous cedar shade.
The drowsy lizard blinks in noon elysium;
A bee clings to the nodding mountain flower
Unfearful o'er the sunlit faëry vale
Far, far below; green isles of tiny trees
Dappling a sea of palpitating sand.

Slow-paced the hours; yet swift the twilight change;
A flare of opal spaces in the west,
Shot with a crimson triumph. Then, the night;
Low call and plaintive answer, till the sheep
Lie bedded round the fire—and Silence dreams.

Star after star is blotted from the mask,
And quick, cool fingers lift the wavering veil
That hangs above the cañon's dusky brim.

The morning hills awake and rise to view
The mesa-reaches sprinkled o'er with bloom;
The Shepherd of the Dawn has loosed his flock
Of silvery sheep to graze celestial pastures,
While, plunging, rears the sun, a golden ram
Who leaps the fiery confines of his fold
Whereon hang curling shreds of snowy fleece
Torn from his eager sides.

             The cañon stream,
Unruffled, bears the aspect of the sky;
Filches a floating cloud that drifts across
The mirrored foliage twinkling in the deep
Cool gardens of its placid underworld.

The dogs are up and out. The shuffling flock
Pours from the bedding-ground, and, grazing, wends
Down to the foot-worn shallows.

             Against the blue
Lone on the height the shepherd hums a song.

# Walkin' John

Walkin' John was a big rope-hoss,
    from over Morongo way;
When you laid your twine on a ragin' steer,
    old John was there to stay.
So long as your rope was stout enough
    and your terrapin shell stayed on,
Dally-welte, or hard-and-fast,
    it was all the same to John.

When a slick-eared calf would curl his tail,
    decidin' he couldn't wait,
Old John, forgettin' the scenery,
    would hit an amazin' gait;
He'd bust through them murderin' cholla spikes,
    not losin' an inch of stride,
And mebbe you wished you was home in bed—
    but, pardner, he made you ride!

Yes, John was willin' and stout and strong,
    sure-footed and Spanish broke,
But I'm tellin' the wonderin' world for once,
    he sure did enjoy his joke;
Whenever the mornin' sun came up
    he would bog his head clear down,
Till your chaps was flappin' like angel wings
    and your hat was a floatin' crown.

That was your breakfast, regular,
    and mebbe you fell or stuck.
At throwin' a whing-ding, John was there
    a-teachin' the world to buck.
But after he got it off his chest
    and the world come back in sight,
He'd steady down like an eight-day clock
    when its innards is oiled and right.

We give him the name of Walkin' John,
    once durin' the round-up time,
Way back in the days when beef was beef
    and John he was in his prime;
Bob was limpin' and Frank was sore
    and Homer he wouldn't talk,
When somebody says, "He's Walkin' John—
    he's makin' so many walk."

But shucks! He was sold to a livery
    that was willin' to take the chance
Of John becomin' a gentleman—
    not scared of them English pants.
And mebbe the sight of them toy balloons
    that is wore on the tourists' legs
Got John a-guessin';
    from that time on he went like he walked on eggs.

As smooth as soap—till a tourist guy,
    bogged down in a pair of chaps,
The rest of his ignorance plumb disguised
    in the rest of his rig—perhaps,
Come flounderin' up to the livery
    and asked for to see the boss:
But Norman he savvied his number right
    and give him a gentle hoss.

Yes, Walkin' John, who had never pitched for a year,
    come first of June.
But I'm tellin' the knock-kneed universe
    he sure recollected soon.
Somebody whanged the breakfast gong,
    though we'd all done had our meat,
And John he started to bust in two,
    with his fiddle between his feet.

That dude spread out like a sailing' bat,
    went floppin' acrost the sky:
He weren't dressed up for to aviate,
    but, sister, he sure could fly!
We picked him out of a cholla bush,
    and some of his clothes staid on;
We felt of his spokes, and wired his folks.
    It was all the same to John.

# The Bosky Steer

Jake and Roany was a-chousin' along,
    And Jake was a-singin' what he called a song,
When up from a waller what should appear,
    But a moss-horned maverick, a bosky steer.

Jake, he started with his hat pulled down,
    Built a blocker that would snare a town;
That steer he headed for the settin' sun,
    And believe me, neighbor, he could hump and run!

Roany he follered his pardner's deal,
    Two ole waddies what could head and heel—
Both of 'em ridin' for the Chicken Coop,
    With a red-hot iron and a hungry loop.

The sun was a-shinin' in ole Jake's eyes,
    And he wasn't just lookin' for no real surprise,
When the steer gave a wiggle like his dress was tight,
    Busted through a juniper and dropped from sight.

Jake and his pony did the figure eight,
    But Jake did his addin' just a mite too late;
He left the saddle, and a-seein' red,
    He lit in the gravel of a river bed.

Now Roany's hoss was a good hoss, too,
    But he didn't understand just why Jake flew,
So he humped and started for the cavvyiard,
    And left Roany settin' where the ground was hard.

Jake was lookin' at a swelled-up thumb,
 And he says, "I reckon we was goin' some!"
When Roany hollers, "Git a-movin' quick,
 Or you're sure goin' to tangle with that maverick!"

Roany clumb a-straddle of the juniper tree.
 "Ain't no more room up here," yells he.
So Jake he figured for hisself to save,
 By backin' in the openin' of a cut-bank cave.

The steer he prodded with his head one side,
 But he couldn't quite make it to ole Jake's hide;
Kep' snortin' and pawin' and proddin' stout,
 But every time he quit, why, Jake come out.

"You ole fool!" yips Roany, "Keep back out of sight!
 You act like you're *hankerin'* to make him fight!"
Then Jake he hollers kinda fierce and queer:
 "Back, hell, nothin'! There's a bear in here!"

# If a Horse Could Talk

I wonder, now, what my pony thinks,
  When I slip his bit and he snuffs and drinks,
  Then noses around the home corral,
  And stands in the corner to rest a spell?

I wonder, now, if he sees the sense
  Of huntin' strays or of mendin' fence?
  Or runnin' stock, or a-ropin' steers,
  Or slittin' a slick-eared yearlin's ears?

Sometimes, when he stands with half-shut eyes,
  Lookin' so solemn and old and wise,
  Just like he savvied the turns and tricks
  Of cows and wimmen and politics,

I get to thinkin' it's just as well,
  Considerin' all that a hoss could tell,
  For me, and many a good cow-hand,
  That a hoss ain't called to the witness-stand.

But speakin' of hangin' and flowers and such,
  Some horses and humans can know too much,
  And get to swellin' and shed their pack,
  A-scatterin' trouble to hell and back.

One time way up by the meadow sink,
  When I was givin' my hoss a drink,
  A city girl on a thoroughbred
  Come ridin' up to the pool and said:

"Why Jim! You here? What a big surprise!"
And she looks at me with them teasin' eyes,
And our horses nickerin' now and then,
Just like they was sayin': "You here again!"

Me leanin' close to her laughin' lips,
When my hoss steps wide and the saddle slips;
Then he bogs his head and he done his best,
And I knew when I lit I was sure Out West.

A-seein'me up in the air like that,
Her hoss stampeded across the flat,
And my pony follows, a-runnin' stout,
And then—a couple of stars come out.

Thinks I, as I started to pull my freight,
"It's six cold miles to the ranchhouse gate,
And a pretty night—for a good, long walk;
How the boys would josh, if a hoss could talk!"

# Toby

Have you ever heard a fellow
    talking nonsense to a hoss,
When he'd stopped to pull a cincha tight
    or take a little rest?
Have you ever seen that same cayuse
    stand looking at his boss
With eyes that seemed to say, "I like you best."

Well, my bronco, little Toby, he had eyes
    that talked like that;
We got pretty well acquainted;
    understood each other right
As we traveled hills and mesas;
    he as nimble as a cat
On the stiffest trail that ever came in sight.

It was: "Toby, come,
    we'll beat it to the reservation line;
Three line-riders over yonder;
    if they see us we're in wrong. . . "
Then the pace that Toby 'd set 'em
    o'er the grass and through the pine,
Made the wind that whistled by sound like a song.

In the camp he'd browse at night
    around his picket, by the fire;
Stop to raise his head
    and watch me like an interested kid;
In the morning he would nicker;
    seemed to say, "Let's take a flyer,
Let's go somewhere";
    and you bet your boots, we did.

Just how much that hoss could sabe,—
　　well, I can't exactly say;
But I told him once of Yuma,
　　the cayuse I left behind
When I hit the dry and dusty
　　coming Arizona way;
Told him she was just another of his kind.

Well, his eyes they did the talking,
　　shining big and round and bright,
Said "I'd like to meet the lady
　　with the blue and glassy eye;
Never been in California,
　　but if you are talking right,
She's a peach; and is she married? Is she shy?"

I told him she was single,
　　fat and pinto,—kind of fair;
Full of ginger and affection
　　that got badly mixed at times;
That she never frizzed her mane
　　or brushed her teeth or combed her hair,
But that she was celebrated in some rhymes.

He seemed quite interested;
　　and her Arizona name
Being "Yuma" set him thinking
　　that my she-cayuse was great;
But he never showed him jealous,
　　being wise and kind and game,
When I talked about our California state.

But since then he's acted offish
   with the hosses on the range;
Nothing mean, but kind of proud-like;
   kept his place and stayed away
From their runs and fights and dinners;
   mebby now you'll think it strange
If I tell you what I heard that Toby say

To the mountain-bred cayuses
   when they dared to ask him why;
"Oh," said Toby, "pretty weather,
   just like California air;
Must excuse me, but a lady
   with a blue and glassy eye—
Boss's friend—is waiting for me, over there."

# Sunlight

Sunlight, a colt from the ranges,
　　glossy and gentle and strong,
Dazed by the multiple thunder
　　of wheels and the thrust of the sea,
Fretted and chafed at the changes—
　　ah, but the journey was long!
Officer's charger—a wonder—
　　pick of the stables was he.

Flutter of flags in the harbor;
　　rumble of guns in the street;
England! and rhythm of marching;
　　mist and the swing of the tide;
France and an Oriflamme arbor of lilies
　　that drooped in the heat;
Sunlight, with mighty neck arching,
　　flecked with the foam of his pride!

Out from the trenches retreating,
　　weary and grimy and worn,
Lean little men paused to cheer him,
　　turning to pass to their rest;
Shrilled him a pitiful greeting,
　　mocking the promise of morn
With hope and wild laughter to hear him
　　answer with challenging zest.

Victory! That was the sprit!
   Once *they* had answered the thrill;
Toiled at the guns while incessant sang
   that invisible, dread
Burden of death. Ah, to hear it,
   merciless, animate, shrill,
Whinning aloft in a crescent,
   shattering living and dead!

And Sunlight? What knew he of battle?
   Strange was this turmoil and haste.
Why should he flinch at the firing;
   swerve at the mangled and slain?
Where was the range and the cattle?
   Here was but carnage and waste;
Yet with a patience untiring
   he answered to spur and to rein.

Answered, when, out of disorder,
   rout, and the chaos of night,
Came the command to his master,
   "Cover the Seventh's retreat!"
On, toward the flame of the border,
   into the brunt of the fight,
Swept that wild wind of disaster,
   on with the tide of defeat.

Softly the dawn-wind
   awaking fluttered a pennant that fell
Over the semblance of Sunlight,
   stark in the pitiless day;
Riddled and slashed by the bullets
   sped from the pit of that hell . . .
Groaning, his master, beside him,
   patted his neck where he lay.

"Sunlight, it wasn't for glory . . .
   England . . . or France . . . or the fame
Of victory . . . No . . .
   not the glowing tribute of history's pen.
Good-bye old chap, for I'm going . . .
   earned it . . . your death is the shame . . .
We fought for the world, not an island.
   We fought for the honor of men."
. . . . . . . . . . . . . . . . . . . . . . . . . . . . . . . .
So we have sold them our horses.
   What shall we do with the gold?
Lay it on Charity's alter,
   purchasing columns of praise?
Noble indeed are our courses;
   running the race as of old;
But why should we Mammonites falter?
   Noble indeed are our ways.

# Old Jim

Black thunder rolled along the mountain-height,
The lightning lashed in whips of burning white
Across the towering pines. Keen, biting, cold
The rain, torrential, smote the mountain-hold:
Quick streams danced down the steep,
   ripped through the trail,
Loosing the tilted rock and hillside shale.

"We can't turn back," the forest ranger said;
So getting from his horse, he slowly led
The way across a narrow, rocky shelf,
A risk for both—yet he went first, himself;
Testing each step to gain the other side,
He heard above the storm the rumbling slide,
Felt the world tremble, dropped the tightened rein,
Then, plunging, rolling, felt a thrust of pain,
Then nothingness.
          Awaking to the day,
Half-buried in the rocky slide he lay,
And knew the freshness of a little breeze;
Saw the bright rain drip slowly from the trees,
Watched the long, western shadows softly fall
Across a sunset-cañon's gilded wall;
Thought of his horse, and summoned will to rise,
Sank back with hot pain branded in his eyes,
Then, with his white lips twisted tense and grim:
"I wonder where the landslide left Old Jim?"

As though in answer to his murmured thought,
He heard the tinkle of a rein-chain; caught
The sound of slipping shale and plodding feet,
Nor ever heard a melody more sweet.
"Jim!" he called hoarsely. "Can you make it, Jim?"
Then, like a dream, his horse limped down to him.
Gashed by the rock and streaked with darkening red
The old horse stood and slowly moved his head,
Nuzzling the limp hand lifted tremblingly,
His great eyes glowing deep with sympathy.
He knew his rider helpless, so he stood,
—A duty taught by toil and hardihood,
The motto of the Service—Loyalty!
"It's up to you to go get help for me":
So spake the ranger. Old Jim seemed to know,
Yet waited for direct command to go.

Down the rude steep, slow plodding through the night
He found his way. He saw the cabin light:
Sniffed at the gate with nostrils round and tense,
Struck with his forefoot at the Station fence,
Then neighed his challenge, loud and high and shrill.
Light-blinded for an instant—stiff and still
He stood.
"Ed's horse!" The valley ranger said:
And then: "The storm—the old cliff-trail—and Ed?"

Without command the old horse led the way
Back through the night to where his rider lay
Pinned by the rock and shale. Thirst-ridden, weak,
Ed heard his name, but had no strength to speak.

"Jim, are you there?" he whispered to the night,
Following with feverish glance the lantern-light,
The shadowy figure laboring at the rock . . .
The clink of steel—and then the sudden shock
Of movement. Oh, the merciful release
Of stupor and an endless dream of peace!

Out of the dream he drifted to the light
Of noonday in the cabin. Swathed in white
He lay, a sorry jest for blithe Romance,
Yet every bit as good a sport as Chance.

He saw the sunlight through the open door,
Saw the far green across the valley floor:
Heard voices in the yard: "The fracture . . . shock . . . "
Then murmured to himself: "You said it, Doc!"

"And he can thank his stars . . ." the voice was grim:
"He's 'way off," murmured Ed. "I'm thankin' Jim."

# Chilao

"Chilao is a gentle hoss."
    That's what his owner told me;
I aimed to buy him from his boss;—
    I reckon that he sold me.
I threw a saddle on the colt
    and forked him, slow and steady,
The owner loosed that thunderbolt,
    then hollered, "Are you ready?"

He kep' his warnin' till the last,
    when I was up—and busy;
That colt he swapped his ends
    so fast he kep' me middlin' dizzy;
I lost one stirrup, popped my hat
    and took to pullin' leather,
Then, him a-kinkin' like a cat,
    we left the earth together.

I raked him where the hair is thin.
    Says I, "That's what I owe you!
The show is on, the folks are in,
    I guess I got to show you!"
He put his nose between his feet
    and humped his back amazin',
Then, when he seen I kep' my seat,
    he quit—and took to grazin'.

Since then he's never kinked a hair:
    as gentle as a kitten.
I reckon if I'd quit him there,
    there'd been no end of quittin'.
He tried it once and made me ride;
    I'll own he had me guessin';
But both of us has kep' our pride—
    and both has learnt a lesson.

He seen that I was there to stay,
    a-comin' or a-goin';
He tried to throw me far away,
    and made a sorry showin';
And when I buy a colt ag'in
    I'll do my own advisin',
And early risin' ain't no sin,
    but not that kind of risin'.

You see, I kep' a saddle warm
    when I was young and limber;
A saplin' 's supple in a storm,
    but not the seasoned timber.
A young tree thinks the wind's a joke—
    and isn't there to take it;
But if a old tree isn't broke,
    a cyclone's like to break it.

But now that: colt, Chilao,
    kind of fancies me, I'm thinkin',
He knows it never slips my mind—
    his eatin' or his drinkin'—
And sometimes, ridin' up from town
    I read the mail I'm packin',
Reins on the horn and hangin' down,
    and he keeps right on shackin'.

And at the gate he's right on deck,
    while I unhook and hook it,
But when you see him arch his neck,
    you'd say he doesn't look it.
It's when you get them playful kind
    and ketch 'em young and growin',
And let 'em know what's in your mind,
    you got the best a-goin'.

Come 'ere, Chilao! Let's shake hands.
    This man, he wants to buy you.
He won't. But sure he understands!
    Now, quit your actin' shy, you!
There's Ma a-callin' us to eat.
    I got more stock to show, sir;
I'll sell 'most anything on feet,
    But not Chilao, no, sir!

# So Long, Chinook!

## (To B. T.)

Chinook, you're free; there's plenty pasture there:
　　Your gallant years have earned you more . . . . and yet. . .
Go on and graze! Don't stand like that and stare!
　　Now quit your nosing! No, I'll not forget.

You want some sugar? Lady's horse you are!
　　I reckon that I've spoiled you. Some would say,
"A pet, that lazies by the corral bar,
　　Rubbing his mane and switching flies all day."

Chinook, they didn't know you as a colt:
　　We were some young and wild those days, Chinook!
They never tamed a foot-loose thunderbolt
　　That pawed a star down, every jump he took.

Here now—my pocket's empty! Drift along,
　　Your saddle's off. Now can't you understand
We've made the last ride, sung the last old song?
　　They signed our warrant when they fenced this land.

Doggone it! This is not a funeral.
　　I've turned you loose for good, old horse; you're free.
Why don't you kick and squeal and act like—well,
　　Perhaps you feel it's tough to quit—like me.

Say, if you will keep nosing me, why, there!
　　Listen! Do you remember how *she* came
Laughing—a rosebud pretty in her hair,
　　And I reached down, And how you played the game?

You, fire and trouble! that day you stood still
　　For once: I was lucky. And that night
I turned you loose to graze on Flores hill:
　　The yucca never bloomed so tall and white!

Young days, young ways, and many trails to ride,
　　And Romance tugging at the bridle-rein:
Chinook, and if we swung a bit aside,
　　We always found the old home trail again.

And here we are! I reckon we're *both* free:
　　No wonder that you stand like that and look
So solemn and so wise. What's wrong with me?
　　I'm talking wild, to-day. So long, Chinook!

# The Walking Man

Sunny summer day it was
    when loping in to Laramie,
I overtook the Walking Man,
    reined up and nodded "How!"
He'd been a rider once, I knew.
    He smiled, but scarce aware of me,
He said, "If you would like me to,
    I'll tell my story now.

"They'll tell you that I'm crazy—
    that my wits have gone to glory,
But you mustn't be believing every
    Western yarn you hear.
The one I'm going to tell you
    is exceptional—a story
That you've heard perhaps a dozen ways
    a dozen times a year."

So he whispered while the shadow
    of my pony walked beside him,
"If good people go to heaven,
    do good horses go to hell?"
I slung one leg across the horn
    and sideways so, I eyed him;
"For I've seen the phantom ponies
    loping round the Big Corral.

"And I've seen my pony Yuma—
    yes, the horse that died to save me—
Come and nicker at the golden bars
    while I stood down below
Calling, 'Yuma! Yuma! Yuma!'
    and still wondering why he gave me
Such a friend; and why I killed her.
    It was twenty years ago . . . .

"You remember; it was lonely when
    we used to guard the cattle;
When a man would ride the line for days
    and camp at night alone,
With nothing much to do but watch
    the sun rise up for battle,
And not a soul to talk to,
    or what's even worse—his own.

"So I taught my pony Yuma many tricks,
    for she was human;
To rear, shake hands, to nod,
    or pick up anything I dropped,

"Till she grew as interested
    and as gentle as a woman,
Just to have me praise and pet her;
    but one day the teaching stopped.

"Three rustlers from the Notch rode up.
    I knew there would be trouble,
But I sat my pony easy
    and I rolled a cigarette,
And we talked about the rodeo,
    when, like a bursting bubble,
The leader opened up the fight.
    I felt my arm grow wet . . . .

"It was three to one; but Yuma,
    like a rock stood to the thunder,
For she seemed to know my need . . . .
    Two empty saddles . . . when the one
That tried at first to get me spurred up close
    and swung up under,
And I saw the trail to heaven
    in the muzzle of his gun.

"I flinched and played the coward.
    'Up!' I called, and at the calling
Reared my pony; and she took his shot.
    I leveled quick and twice
I answered. In the smoke
    I saw a twisted figure falling;
I could feel my pony shiver . . . .
    Twenty years I've paid the price

"For my life. Yes,
    Hell-and-Texas leave the hoof prints
        in some faces;
We, the riders of the ranges,
    each of us has played his part . . . .
Twenty years!" he whispered slowly.
    "Twenty years in many places,
But I've never worn the print
    of Yuma's hoof-marks from my heart.

"I'm the Walking Man forever.
    But I dream of mighty ranges
And the silent mountain-meadows
    in the glory of the stars;
And I see the phantom ponies
    in the dawn and sunset changes,
And I hear my Yuma nicker,
    just behind the golden bars."

Sunny summer day it was
    when loping in to Laramie,
I overtook the Walking Man,
    reined up and nodded "How!"
He walked beside me for awhile.
    He hardly was aware of me,
But I think I understand him,
    For I know his story now.

# Oliver West

Oliver West came riding down;
   His face was lean and keen and brown,
And his eyes were fixed on the desert town
   At the end of the Sunset Trail.

Without the ghost of a good excuse,
   He set his spurs in his roan cayuse,
"Lay to it, Sarko! Cut her loose!"
   And the pebbles flew like hail.

"Hi! Yip! I can hear the silver strings,
   And the song that the little Bonita sings;
Say, Sarko, I wish that your feet were wings,
   But you're doin' your best, all right!"

The sun rolled down to the western range,
   And he watched the shadows shift and change,
And the little lights of the town looked strange
   As they beckoned across the night.

An hour—and he clinked to the doorway glare
   Of the 'dobe. The singing girl was there,
With a southern rose in her midnight hair,
   And lips like a bud of June.

"Onda, La Onda," the song began,
   As softly the silver music ran
To the heart of the swart El Capitan,
   'T was the Gringo lover's tune.

The little Bonita saw and smiled,
  With the pouting lips of a teasing child;
She loved—but the Gringo was not beguiled;
  'T was a heart that she could not tame.

A word—and the swell of the music broke;
  The room was a pit of flame and smoke,
But Oliver West not a word he spoke,
  As into the night he came.

Then with more than the ghost of a good excuse,
  He set his spurs in his roan cayuse;
"Lay to it, Sarko! Hell's broke loose!"
  And the pebbles flew like hail.

"Onda, La Onda's a right good song,"
  Said Oliver West as he loped along;
"Was it he or she or me done wrong?
  Well, she's there—and I'm here,
    and we're goin' strong,
Back over the Sunset Trail."

# The Oro Stage

Around the bend we streaked it
  with the leaders swingin' wide;
    Round the bend and down the mountain
    from the old El Oro mines:
Jim Waring he was ridin' gun—
  a sawed-off at his side,
    And the sun was settin' level through the pines.
      We was late—and come a-reelin',
      With the gritty brakes a-squealin',
    And the slack a-dancin' lively down the lines.

Jim Waring he said nothin',
  for he weren't the talkin' kind;
    He left that to his lawyer—and his lawyer was a gun;
But I seen as plain as daylight
  he had somethin' on his mind,
    'Cause he kept a-glancin' sideways at the sun:
      And we hit the grade a—glidin',
      With the smokin' tires a—slidin',
    Then I give the broncs a chanct, and let 'em run.

And them broncs was doing noble—
  layin' clost and reachin' far,
    With the Concord chains a-snappin'
    and the brakes a-swingin' free,
And the Notch below a-loomin'
  plumb ag'inst the evenin' star,
    And nothin' in the road that I could see:
      Stage a-rollin'—hosses reekin',
      With the heavin' springs a-squeakin'
    When Jim Waring touched me
    gentle with his knee.

Oh, I knowed just what was comin'.
  We was packin' Oro dust—
    And that hombre there beside me
    didn't know what quittin' meant:
We was bustin' on a hold-up.
  It was Salvador, or bust:
    With our chanct of winnin'
    worth about a cent:
        Now I weren't no outlaw stopper,
        But I sure could shoot the popper,
    So I shot it to the broncs—and in we went.

I seen a bridle shinin'
  and a shadder in the brush,
    Then a streak of red come flittin'
    and a-spittin' through the black:
I seen a empty saddle
  in the ruckus and the rush,
And the leaders pawin' air, and traces slack.
        Hell it sure was loose and hoppin'
        With Jim Waring's gun a-poppin',
    And a-spreadin' his ideas in his track.

If the game was worth the glory,
  then we ought to had a crown,
    For we sure was nominated,
    biddin' high for all we got:
I was watchin' of the hosses
  when I seen Jim's gun come down,
    And I smelt the powder-smoke a-blowin' hot,
        As we took the grade a-flyin'
        With the pinto wheeler dyin'
    And Jim doin' business every time he shot.

We made it! And the wind was fannin' cool
  ag'inst my face:
    But the scare was still a-boilin'
    where I aim to keep my brains:
The wheeler he was weavin'
  and a-saggin' on the trace,
When San Salvador loomed up acrost the plains
      And we hit the town a-reelin',
        With the gritty brakes a-squealin',
     And the pinto wheeler draggin' in the chains.

# Charley Lee

A low moon shone on the desert land
    and the sage was silver white,
As Lee—a thong round hand and hand—
    stood straight in the lantern light.
  "You have strung up Red and Burke," said he,
  "And you say that the next will be Charley Lee,
  But there's never a rope was made for me."
And he laughed in the quiet night.

They shaped the noose and
    they flicked the rope, and over the limb it fell,
And Charley Lee saw the ghost of hope
    go glimmering down to hell.
  Two shadows swung from the cottonwood tree,
  And the wind went whispering, "Charley Lee,"
  For the turning shadows would soon be three,
And never a stone to tell.

"Have ye more to say for yourself?" said Gray,
    "a message the like, or prayer?
If ye have, then hasten and have your say.
    We trailed and we trapped ye fair,
  With fire and iron at Hidden Sink,
  Where none but the stolen horses drink.
  And the chain but wanted a final link.
Ye were riding my red roan mare."

"But prove your property first," said Lee.
   "Would you call the mare your own,
With never a brand or mark to see,
   or name to the big red roan?
  But strip the saddle and turn her loose,
  And I'll show that the mare is my own cayuse.
  And I don't—then take it a fair excuse,
To tighten the rope you've thrown."

Gaunt, grim faces and steady eyes
   were touched with a somber look,
And hands slipped slowly to belted thighs
   and held on a finger-crook,
  For Gray of Mesa who claimed the mare,
  Had talked too much as he led them there,
  No other among them knew the lair,
So a grip on their haste they took. . .

"Give him a chance," said Monty Wade,
   and, "What is the use?" said Blake.
"He's done," said Harney; "his string is played.
   But we'll give him an even break."
  So they led the mare to the cottonwood tree,
  Nor saddle nor bridle nor rope had she.
  "Bonnie, come here!" said Charley Lee,
And soft was the word he spake.

The roan mare came and she nosed his side
   and nuzzled him friendly-wise;
"Kneel!" cried Lee, and he leaped astride
   and fled as the swallow flies.
  Flashes followed his flight in vain,
  Bullets spattered the ground like rain,
  Hoofs drummed far on the midnight plain,
And a low moon rode the skies.

Dawn broke red on the desert land
   where the turning shadows fell,
And the wind drove over the rolling sand
   with a whimpering ebb and swell,
  Whispering, whispering, "Charley Lee,"
  As south on the red roan mare rode he,
  Yet the turning shadows they were three,
And never a stone to tell.

# The Rustler

From the fading smoke of a branding-fire
    in a mesquite hollow close and dim,
We followed a phantom pony-track,
    over the range and down
Into the cool, deep cañon gloom,
    then up to the mesa's ragged rim;
And the foam-clots flew from our swinging reins
    as we loped to the desert town.

Gray in the dusk at the hitching-rail
    there loomed the shape of a lean cayuse,
His gaunt flanks streaked with dust-dried sweat
    in the doorway's golden glow;
A rider stood at the lamplit bar
    tugging the knot of his neck-scarf loose,
And some one sang to the silver strings
    in the moonlit patio.

He flung a coin as we crowded in.
    He knew us all, but with no surprise:
We had run him down and he faced us square,
    a fighter from hat to heel:
The music stopped and a Spanish girl
    came from the dusk, her wondering eyes
Filled with a strange and fearsome light;
    but his were as cool as steel.

Tense as a lion crouched to spring
    he poised on the midnight brink of fate;
But she, with a smile, drew near the lamp,
    playing the woman's game:
A crash—and the room was black and still:
    a whispered word and we knew, too late,
As hell surged up in our hearts, we drew
    and the dark was streaked with flame.

We heard the thud of a pony's stride
    and shuffled back to the open door,
Ringed by a sudden crowd that came,
    questioning, shuffling, till
A light was made in the 'dobe bar,
    and a shadow lay on the beaten floor—
We saw an arm and an upturned face,
    girlish and white and still.

Gray in the dusk at the hitching-rail
    there loomed the shape of a lean cayuse,
His gaunt flanks streaked with sun-dried sweat
    in the lamplight's golden glow:
But no rider stood at the lamplit bar
    tugging the knot of his neck-scarf loose,
And no one sang to the silver strings
    in the moonlit patio.

## Bill Tandy

Bill Tandy, ridin' Hell's Delight,
 come foggin' into town one night,
With three months' wages in his jeans,
 a clean shirt in his slicker.
"Three months of cows and alkali,"
 says he, "would make a angel dry!
I got no wings, but watch me fly!"
 And then he took some liquor.

Now Bill warn't bad, but plenty wild
 when red-eye got his feelin's riled,
And then he gets some careless
 with his language and his gun;
He mounts that little roan cayuse
 and whoops and turns the fireworks loose,
A-spurrin' up and down the street
 and shootin' on the run.

Three times he comes a streakin' red
and everybody duckin' lead,
With window lights a-poppin' out
and glass a-rattlin' down.
We kind of liked to see him play
and so we let him have his way,
For, Stranger, I admire to say
he livened up the town.

He ventilated signs and doors
and like to ruined dance-hall floors,
A-shootin' heels off slippers
and a-scarin' of the girls;
Him figurin' they was hard to please
he dusted the piano keys
A-tryin' to play "My Rosary"—
but he busted all the pearls.

There come a time he got so tough
we figured he had played enough,
And so the sheriff warned him,
kind of easy-like and slow:
"You're gettin' too expensive, Bill.
Just curl your tail and climb the hill."
But Bill he says, "Like hell I will!
I'm set. Just watch me go!"

The sheriff aimed to run the town,
so he just knocked Bill Tandy down,
And easin' him of belt and gun
he throwed him into jail;
But Bill come to at twelve that night,
broke jail, and mounted Hell's Delight,
And thinkin' he warn't treated right
he hit the sheriff's trail.

Us settin' in a poker game, the sheriff says,
    "This here is tame,
I'll raise you"—when Bill Tandy
    spurred his pony through the door;
Well, we-all didn't see no joke
    in settin' still and eatin' smoke,
So four of us we up and spoke,
    and Bill he hit the floor.

Which done, we-all set down again.
    The sheriff says, "I'll raise you ten."
Buck Yardlaw calls, the sheriff shows
    and gathers in the pot.
The crowd come back. We passed the hat;
    bought Bill a suit—he needed that,
And planted him on Alder Flat—
    a mighty pretty spot.

# Yardlaw's Ride

The high stream gnawed at the river-bank
    And the dead clay crumbled down,
As the snow fed current flung its mane
    with a charging leap and toss,
When, roweled red from cinch to flank
    in a midnight race from town,
A big roan plunged in the yellow flood
    and battled his way across.

Yardlaw bent to the sound of rain
    as he paused on the farther shore,
Flung a glance in the night behind,
    peered in the night ahead,
Felt the ribs of the red roan strain
    as he gathered breath once more,
Then a quick-crooked knee as the steel bit in
    And over the trail he fled.

Into the blind, black face of night
    he flung on his fearsome way,
Gathered tense for a stumbling lurch,
    a hoof on a turning stone,
A foreleg snapped, perchance, then fight!
    And he visioned a wolf at bay,
As mile after mile was spurned behind
    by the hoofs of the big red roan.

South and south to the open land,
    south to the viewless line,
Battered stiff by the slanting storm
    that scattered the sand afar,
Yardlaw fled from a capture planned
    by the men of the Nine-Bar-Nine,
And the grim, gray face of the man he'd killed,
    That night, at the Oro Bar.

The big red roan knew naught of this
    as he swung to the level plain,
Yet he knew that Fear in the saddle sat
    and hot Hate followed fast;
He flinched as he heard a thirty hiss
    like the stinging lash of rain,
Yet lost no inch of his running reach
    as the night wind hurtled past.

Dawn lay on the Rim like a golden rope
    round yucca and sage and sand,
As Yardlaw, sparing a glance behind,
    loosened his saddle gun,
And pulled the roan to an easy lope,
    as he gazed at the desert land,
Seeking a hollow to make his fight
    with his back to the rising sun.

They came in the flame of the desert day,
    out of the empty night,
Three riders far on a little rise,
    and Yardlaw raised his head;
He saw a shimmering black dot
    play on his sun-blurred rifle sight,
Then the whip of a slug that snarled through space:
    "They've a horse to spare," he said.

Wide they rode of the water-hole,
    circled the desert wide,
Two black dots where there had been three;
    and Yardlaw knew their play,
And made his own as he slowly stole
    to the top of the low divide,
Swung to the roan and headed south
    in the heat of the naked day.

A bullet tugged at his open sleeve
    and he heard the distant shot,
Turned in the saddle, replied in kind,
    then dropped like a falling stone,
Playing his desperate make-believe—
    and whether they knew or not,
He took the chance as he watched
    the ears and the eye of the big red roan.

An hour in the burning silence vast,
    and the red roan's gallant head
Drooped to the thrust of the desert sun.
    Weary and worn he stood,
Knowing now he could rest at last,
    for Hate to the north had sped;
Buck Yardlaw rose and loosed the cinch
    and cursed at the solitude.

# Song of Mercado

Just over the border where strife and disorder
    Make living a difficult trade,
The bandit, Mercado, his watchword "Cuidado!"
    Delighted to pillage and raid.

And each ragged fellow who didn't show yellow
    Was given a chance to recruit,
Or lacking ambition soon took the position
    Inspired by the simple word "Shoot!"

With followers twenty and vino aplenty,
    This sprightly Fulano de Tal
Stole horses and chickens and stirred up the dickens
    From Alamos down to Parral;

Then riding like thunder he'd fly with his plunder,
    And hide in the heart of the range,
Where weary of sticking and thieving and picking
    He'd pick the guitar for a change.

"When young I wore leather and gold,
    A hunter of thieves—a *rural*,
And now I am hunted. Behold,
    I follow Fulano de Tal!

"My friend is my little carbine,
    A trusty companion is she;
My foe is the man in between
    His sack of *dinero* and me.

"I raid and I plunder the great,
    And much to the lowly I give;
When *pesos* are plenty, why wait?
    *Por dios!* a fellow must live!

"The valley for forage and loot,
    The hills for the hunted ladron;
High life and hot liquor to boot,
    And every man out for his own.

"Yet beware of the *portal azul*,
    And too much *Bonita* at home;
A lover is ever a fool,
    And love is a kettle of foam.

"I take what I need when I will,
    I drink till the bottle is dry;
Though Fate bring good fortune or ill,
    *Por dios!* a fellow must die!

"So beware of the liquor that's free,
    Red wine is the advocate's ink;
And beware, my *bandidos*, of me!
    *Por dios!* but hand me a drink!"

Thus Manuel Mercado with tuneful bravado,
    A Spanish guitar in his hand,
Sang gayly of bullets, gold, liquor, and pullets,
    To please his illiterate band;

And when Time took a hitch in his open-air kitchen,
    He'd lay his guitar in the shade,
And with brisk dots and dashes he'd curl his moustaches,
    And take up the tools of his trade.

## Boomer Johnson

Now Mr. Boomer Johnson
    was a gettin' old in spots,
But you don't expect a bad-man
    to go wrastlin' pans and pots;
But he'd done his share of killin'
    and his draw was gettin' slow,
So he quits a-punchin' cattle
    and he takes to punchin' dough.

Our foreman up and hires him,
    figurin' age had rode him tame,
But a snake don't get no sweeter
    just by changin' of its name.
Well, Old Boomer knowed his business—
    he could cook to make you smile,
But say, he wrangled fodder
    in a most peculiar style.

He never used no matches—
    left 'em layin' on the shelf;
Just some kerosene and cussin'
    and the kindlen' lit itself.
And, pardner, I'm allowin'
    it would give a man a jolt,
To see him stir *frijoles*
    with the barrel of his Colt.

Now killin' folks and cookin'
    ain't so awful far apart;
That must 'a' been why
    Boomer kept a-practicin' his art;
With the front sight of his pistol
    he would cut a pie-lid slick,
And he'd crimp her with the muzzle
    for to make the edges stick.

He built his doughnuts solid,
    and it sure would curl your hair,
To see him plug a doughnut
    as he tossed it in the air.
He bored the holes plumb center
    every time his pistol spoke
Till the can was full of doughnuts
    and the shack was full of smoke.

We-all was gettin' jumpy—
    but he couldn't understand
Why his shootin' made us nervous
    when his cookin' was so grand.
He kept right on performin',
    and it weren't no big surprise,
When he took to markin' tombstones
    on the covers of his pies.

They didn't taste no better
    and they didn't taste no worse,
But a-settin' at that table
    was like ridin' in a hearse;
You didn't do no talkin'
    and you took just what you got,
So we et till we was foundered
    just to keep from gettin' shot.

Us at breakfast one bright morning,
    I was feelin' kind of low,
When Old Boomer passed the doughnuts
    and I tells him plenty, "No!
All I takes this trip is coffee,
    for my stomach is a wreck,"
I could see the itch for killin'
    swell the wattles on his neck.

Scorn his grub! He strings some doughnuts
    on the muzzle of his gun,
And he shoves her in my gizzard
    and he says, "You're takin' one!"
He was set to start a graveyard,
    but for once he was mistook;
Me not wantin' any doughnuts,
    I just up and salts the cook.

Did they fire him? Listen, pardner,
    there was nothin' left to fire.
Just a row of smilin' faces
    and another cook to hire.
If he joined some other outfit
    and is cookin'—what I mean,
It's where they ain't no matches
    and they don't need kerosene.

# Ballad of Billy the Kid

No man in the West ever won such renown
As young Billy Bonney of Santa Fe town,
And of all the wild outlaws that met a bad end,
None so quick with a pistol or true to a friend.

It was in Silver City his first trouble came,
A man called Billy's mother a very foul name;
Billy swore to get even, his chance it came soon,
When he stabbed that young man in Joe Dyer's saloon.

He kissed his poor mother and fled from the scene,
A bold desperado and not yet fifteen;
He hid in a sheep-camp but short was his stay,
For he stole an old pony and rode far away.

At monte and faro he next took a hand,
And lived in Tucson on the fat of the land;
But the game was too easy, the life was too slow,
So he drifted alone into Old Mexico.

It was not very long before Billy came back,
With a notch in his gun and some gold in a sack;
He struck for the Pecos his comrades to see,
And they all rode to Lincoln and went on a spree.

There he met his friend Tunstall and hired as a hand
To fight with the braves of the Jingle-bob brand;
Then Tunstall was murdered and left in his gore;
To avenge that foul murder Young Billy he swore.

First Morton and Baker he swiftly did kill,
Then he slaughtered Bill Roberts at Blazer's sawmill;
Sheriff Brady and Hindman in Lincoln he slew,
Then he rode to John Chisum's along with his crew.

There he stood off a posse and drove them away.
In McSween's house in Lincoln he made his next play;
Surrounded he fought till the house was burned down,
But he dashed through the flames and escaped from the town.

Young Billy rode north and Young Billy rode south,
He plundered and killed with a smile on his mouth,
But he always came back to Fort Sumner again
For his Mexican sweetheart was living there then.

His trackers were many, they followed him fast,
In Arroyo Tivan he was captured at last;
He was taken to Lincoln and put under guard,
And sentenced to hang in the old court-house yard.

J. Bell and Bob Ollinger watched day and night,
And Bob told Young Billy he'd made his last fight.
Young Billy gave Olinger scarcely a glance,
But sat very still and awaited his chance.

One day he played cards with J. Bell in the room,
Who had no idea how close was his doom;
Billy slipped off a handcuff, hit Bell on the head.
Then he snatched for the pistol and shot him down dead.

Bob Ollinger heard and he ran to the spot
To see what had happened and who had been shot;
Young Billy looked down from a window and fired,
Bob Ollinger sank to the ground and expired.

Then Young Billy escaped on a horse that was near,
As he rode forth from Lincoln he let out a cheer;
Though his foes they were many he feared not a one,
So long as a cartridge remained in his gun.

But his comrades were dead or had fled from the land,
It was up to Young Billy to play a lone hand;
And Sheriff Pat Garrett he searched far and wide,
Never thinking the Kid in Fort Sumner would hide.

But when Garrett heard Billy was hiding in town,
He went to Pete Maxwell's when the sun had gone down;
The door was wide open, the night it was hot,
So Pat Garrett walked in and sat down by Pete's cot.

Young Billy had gone for to cut him some meat,
No hat on his head and no boots on his feet;
When he saw two strange men on the porch in the gloom,
He pulled his gun quick and backed into the room.

Billy said, "Who is that?" and he spoke Maxwell's name,
Then from Pat Garrett's pistol the answer it came—
The swift, cruel bullet went true to its mark,
And Young Billy fell dead on the floor in the dark.

So Young Billy Bonney he came to his end,
Shot down by Pat Garrett who once was his friend;
Though for coolness and courage both gunmen ranked high,
It was Fate that decided Young Billy should die.

Each year of his life was a notch in his gun,
For in twenty-one years he had slain twenty-one.
His grave is unmarked and by desert sands hid,
And so ends the true story of Billy the Kid.

# Sandy Rue

A gray horse in the moonlight,
    a shadow on the wall;
Like laughter of a soul bewitched,
    a far coyote's call;
Three horsemen drew beside the gate
    that took the doorway light,
And one he called for Sandy Rue
    to ride with them the night.

"It's long we've had a word of you
    and far we made the ride,
We've waited by The Burning Hill
    and by the river-side,
Not once have you come back
    to curse the places where we died."

Another spoke—
    and Sandy Rue put hand upon the gray,
And fumbling gave the horse the bit,
    nor had a word to say,
As: "So you saddled in the night
    and rode to shoot me down,
And still you bear a killer's name
    in old Sonora-town."

"It's long we've had a word of you;
    Chiquita's mouth is cold;
Forgotten is the song she sang,
    the secret that she told,
Yet you remember, Sandy Rue,
    the sin you did for gold."

Another voice—
    and Sandy Rue drew leather through the ring,
And pulled the cincha, made the tie,
    and gave the rein a fling:
His boot was to the stirrup; then,
    "You've not forgot the knack,
As when we crossed the San Gorgone,
    but only one came back.

"It's long from here to San Gorgone,
    where you let me lie
Beside the empty water-hole,
    beneath a burning sky,
Your sin the promise that you gave—
    and left me there to die."

Then spoke the first, as Sandy Rue,
    with swift and cunning hand,
Drew gun and fired at phantom things
    that gave the dark command;
While spent the shots were lost in space
    that whistled to their flight,
"Put by the gun and mount your horse;
    you ride with us, the night."

The cabin window-panes
    were red with dawn across the hill,
And Sandy's cat was curled
    against the sunlit window-sill,
And Sandy Rue had gone to join the ghosts
    he could not kill.

Beyond his cramped and wasted hand
    lay Sandy's empty gun,
And so a rancher found him,
    stark, beneath the desert sun,
Yet not a mark of harm to show,
    or trace of those who ride,
For trackless are the phantom trails
    across The Great Divide.

So evil turned upon itself
    and slew the thing it made;
And simple praise was on the stone
    where Sandy Rue was laid,
And kindly hearts with desert flowers
    his lonely grave arrayed.

# Eh, Johnny-Jo?

Just turn me loose on them hills a spell!
    Hear the rein-chains jingle and saddle creak?
And after chuck, that there pack-horse bell
    'Way off, jing-janglin'; hear it speak?
Say, a minute of that is worth a week
    In town. . . . And the wind is driftin' slow,
A-pilin' the sand round the chaparral
    And them dam' coyotes singin' all
Together.
                It's great, ain't it, Johnny-Jo?

But, whoa! I must shine up my langwidge some,
    This ain't no round-up; this here is verse
That's a-lopin' along and it's got to come,
    Like the parson says, "For good or worse."
So I'll clamp my knees and just let her hum.

The wind of the dawn has swept the plains,
    And the sun runs over the purple sage.
Gone is the wrack of the winter rains,
    Leaving the hills like a faëry page
Of a book that is old, but is ever new,
    And fresh as the wild-flowers sweet with dew . . .
Gosh! I'm ridin' close to the fence and low,
    And strainin' my buttins, eh, Johnny-Jo?

It ain't no use for to talk like that;
    It's second-hand scenery made to print.
Just hand me my ole gray puncher hat
    And them spurs and quirt; do you get the hint?
For I *got* to ride easy with elbows high,
    Mebby not style, but she sure has go;
We'll all git to Heaven by-and-by,
    But we'll travel outdoors; eh, Johnny-Jo?

# On the Range

My pony was standin' thinkin' deep;
    Can hosses think? Well, I reckon so!
And I was squattin', half asleep,
    When into the firelight stepped a Bo.

He grinned in a kind of friendly way;
    He ate some grub and he rolled a smoke.
I sort of listened for him to say
    What was comin'—and this is how he spoke:

"Oh, the world is good and her towns are good,
    And so are her folks, if understood.
Hay-foot, straw-foot, left and right,
    Over the next hill, out of sight,
Rambling everywhere, day and night,
    And plenty of things to see;

"For the world is good and her folks are good,
    And all of 'em like to be understood,
From the rich man ridin' his limousine
    To the guy that is hit by the big machine,
And the thousand or so that are in between,
    Clear down to a Bo, like me.

"All you have to do is to cast your eye
    On the sun or the stars, without askin' why,
Or the moon there, rollin' above the line;
    She don't crowd the stars but she lets 'em shine:
And pal, don't you think they are doin' fine,
    All helpin' to make the show?

"And we all got passes to go and see
    All there is—and all there is goin' to be.
Hay-foot and straw-foot, left and right,
    And I'm usin' my pass both day and night,
And she's good for the whole show. Get me right?
    And I'm nothin' except a Bo;

"Yes, the coarsest siftin' of the lot.
    Now imagine the chance that best has got.
Sure there ain't no medals stuck on my vest,
    But I wouldn't change with the gilt-edged best,
And when it comes time to lie down and rest,
    Well I guess it will come right good;

"But somehow, or somehow to *me*, it seems
    That that pass is good where they make the dreams.
Say, maybe we'll see it all over again,
    The wind and the sun and the snow and rain,
And old friends and places, and see 'em plain,
    And *all* of 'em understood."

I was punchin' then for the old Tejon.
    *I* reckon I won't forget that night,
Or the Bo and me by the fire alone,
    With nothin' but sand and sage in sight.

169

# Apuni Oyis

## (Butterfly Lodge)

There's a lodge in Arizona
    where the rugged pines are marching
Straight and stalwart up the hillside
    till they gather on the crest,
And around their feet the grasses
    and the purple flowers are arching
In the dim and golden glamour
    of the sunlight in the West.

In the lodge—Apuni Oyis dwells
    the Chief who writes the stories
Of the Blackfeet mighty hunters
    in the pleasant days of old—
Tales of love and war and friendship,
    tales of mysteries and glories,
When the prairie moon was silver
    and the sun was faëry gold.

And the trails along the mountains,
    o'er the mesa and the river,
Lead to far and hidden cañons
    where the sleeping red men lie,
Wrapped in silence
    as above them myriad aspen leaves aquiver
Whisper secrets to the west wind
    as the pack-train ambles by;

Where the swart Apache hunts and dreams
    of warriors now a-dreaming;
Where the mountain stream runs swiftly,
    talking loudly to the day,
To the rock-rimmed pool
    and onward as an unexpected gleaming
Marks the trout that leaps
    to vanish in a burst of silver spray:

Trails that climb the rocky fortress of the ridge
    and have their ending
In forlorn and ravaged temples
    of a people all unknown;
Trails we make, and did we know it—
    on and on forever blending
With the red man's, toward the sunset—
    are no clearer than his own.

Oh, the hills of Arizona
    in the pleasant autumn weather!
Oh, the lodge—Apuni Oyis—
    where is happiness and rest!
May the dreams we share come true,
    and may we live them all together,
We who love the ancient magic
    of the mountains of the West.

# Down Along the Dim Trail

Down along the dim trail, far across the plain,
Rode a waddie singing, heedless of the rain
Rattling on his slicker and dripping from his hat,
Gnawing at the cut-banks and spreading on the flat:

> *"Wrangle up the parson, don't forget the ring:*
> *Throw your fancy saddle on the old red-roan:*
> *If you 're feelin' lonesome, shake yourself and sing,*
> *When your girl is waitin', down in San Antone."*

Gloomy were the tall sticks, gusty was the night,
Mournful was the hoot owl calling from the height,
Chilly was the bed-roll, slender was the flame,
But the happy puncher kept a-singing just the same:

> *"Eighty miles behind me and forty more to go,*
> *Forkin' from the old trail and figurin' my own:*
> *Baldy's doin' noble—but noble's mighty slow,*
> *When your girl is waitin', down in San Antone."*

Trailing from the high peaks ran the morning mist;
Far below, the desert shone like amethyst;
Golden was the dim trail, glowing was the day,
Just the kind of weather for singing on the way:

> *"Yonder lies the old town, loomin' on the sky,*
> *Sleepy as a lizard dreamin' on a stone:*
> *If you was an eagle, mebby-so you'd fly,*
> *When your girl is waitin', down in San Antone."*

Someone saw the rider long before he came;
Someone picked a red rose, someone breathed a name.
Lowered were her dark eyes, bashful, young, and sweet,
When she heard a faint song winging down the street:

> *"Mebby-so I'm dreamin', mebby-so it's me,*
> *And someone in the sunshine, watchin' all alone—*
> *Seem your eyes git blurry, like you couldn't see,*
> *When your girl is waitin', down in San Antone."*

# The Ranger and the Bear

Up in the high Sierras,
    where they overlook the Kern,
There's a trail on the edge of nothing,
    and a mile by the plumb below,
Is a tomb for the upland rider
    that is fool enough to turn
His hoss till he reaches the meadows beyond
    where the mountain-daisies grow.

The sun was painting the eastern peaks
    with a kind of running fire,
But a morning chill was in the air
    as keen as an eagle's claw;
I was riding slouched and easy-like
    and singing of heart's desire,
When my pony stopped, though the rein was slack,
    and my singing stopped; I saw

Black on the cliff a something bigger
    than any man;
Blur . . .'twas a old she-grizzly
    blocking the trail ahead;
She talked to the cubs beside her
    and they turned at her growl and ran
As my hand slid down to my holster;
    but I changed my mind; instead

I, off of my hoss, stepped forward
    and raising my hat polite
(But I raised my hat left-handed,
    my right being filled and pat)
I said to that old bear-lady:
    "Now it isn't my wish to fight,
Or I'd set to fanning my six-gun
    'stead of tipping to you my hat."

And, pardner, would you believe it!
    she dropped to the ledge and swung . . .
Turned where a hoss couldn't make it
    and took after them cubs of hern;
I stood there looking foolish
    where a bunch of them blue flowers hung
Over the edge of nothing,
    smiling down on the river Kern.

My cayuse was a-shaking and sweating;
    he was chilly—and so was I,
Howcome, I swung to the saddle
    and got him a-moving slow,
But I quit my glass-eyed gazing
    at the colors across the sky
And took to surveying the landscape just ahead,
    where we had to go.

Mebby a half-hour later
    we was pushing across the line
Where the rock joins on to the timber
    when I spied a few rods away
The back of that old she-grizzly;
    I went for that gun of mine;
Then, thinks I, *she* is minding her business;
    so I'll tend to my own, to-day.

Just a-guarding her headstrong young ones;
    doing the best she can;
Willing to do the wise thing;
    game, but not looking for fight;
Pretty good rule for a human . . .
    Oh, I guess I'm an easy man,
But the grizzly and me broke even,
    'cause the both of us was polite.

# The Prospector

'Tis the wane of the moon
    and the midsummer revels are ended,
And Autumn has burnished the vale
    with an indolent hand;
And the breeze of the morn
    with the breath of adventuring blended,
Wakes a song in my heart
    as I dream of a far-away land.

So I'll up with the sun
    while the city is torpid in slumber;
Let the wind wash the reek
    of the factory smoke from my clothes;
For I've worked like a stamp in the mill
    leaden days without number,
And I'm off to the land
    where the bloom of the almond-tree blows.

To the land of the West,
    where the blue, where the ultimate ranges
Sun their cloud-muffled shoulders
    and sit with their feet in the sea;
Where the way of the world drifts along
    without too many changes,
And a man without money has friends—
    if he cares to be free.

With the little I'll have when I get there
    I'll buy me a pony,
A pinto cayuse that knows trails
    and the trick of the rope,
And he'll be my singular,
    faithful old stand-by and crony
When we're tired of the valley
    we'll cinch up and ride for the slope.

We will camp on the crest of the foothills
    that run to the mountains,
On the side where the sun disappears
    down the slope of the sea;
And we'll watch as the tide
    shatters sky-ward in thundering fountains,
While the stars find their places
    and shine through the sycamore tree.

We will follow the song of the meadow-lark
    out to the grazing;
The dim mountain meadow,
    knee-deep with the greenest of grass,—
Or we'll creep round the ledge
    where the little red wildflower is blazing
And drop down to Eden
    and trot through the Porcupine Pass.

Call it prospecting, loafing, surveying,
    or simply just living,
Never think it's the lure of the gold
    that keeps calling me on;

Merely taking the gifts mother nature
    to all men is giving,
Yes, even the last, the long rest,
    with a smile. When I'm gone . . . .

When I'm gone? Well, the mountains are monuments
    grander than glory;
And a cañon's a tomb
    that's as noble as any they've made.
Let the eagle that feathers the blue
    tell the ocean the story,
When the pinto strays
    dragging a rope down the Porcupine grade.

Call it prospecting? Maybe it is.
    And I know when it's ended,
And I climb the Divide
    and report on the use of my claim,
I won't get much credit
    for anything noble or splendid;
But He knows why I turned from the town
    to the open-air game.

# Songs of Men

To please the pale, aesthetic mind
    is not our chief desire or hope,
Nor yet to charm the woman's ear
    who comes upon this rhyme by chance;
Our song is loud we-all allow,
    of spur and rifle, horse and rope,
Of trail and trouble, wind and sun,
    and many a crimson circumstance.

You'll find no noble sentiment,
    although in every verse you look;
Nor classic melody entwined
    about a theme of sob or sigh;
But like the rest we up and went and saw,
    and what we saw, we took
To monument our glory-trail
    and leave a name to know us by.

We partners bought a horse apiece
    and learned how far a man may fall
And rise again without the aid of crutches,
    splints, or angel wings;
We learned to save the bacon grease
    and flop the flapjack, large or small:
To ride and shoot and punch the dough—
    drink alkali, and other things.

We learned to throw the diamond hitch
   and swim a ford grown impolite;
To rope and tally, brand and cut
   the steer we wanted from the herd:
To never call a man a name
   unless we were prepared to fight;
This rhyme internal staggers—
   but you're welcome to supply the word.

We traveled high, we traveled far,
   and found a trail or made our own;
Ate tough tortillas in the heat
   or thawed our grub at Fifty-Three;
We dallied at The Klondike bar,
   or played the wheel in San Antone;
We locked the door on Vain Regret
   and, poco pronto, lost the key.

We crossed the border,
   drifting down to dark Sonora in the South;
Bought trinkets for the Spanish girls—
   and ammunition on the side—
Made love in old Sonora town
   and kissed Romance upon the mouth;
Blew out a Chola light or two—
   and then we simply *had* to ride.

We paid to hear the bottles pop;
   and paid for silk, chiffon, and lace;
Wore tans and gaiters, tinted socks,
   and graced the sidewalks of New York;
Got pinched at Maxim's—bribed the cop,
   but never learned to quite outface
The early morning looking-glass—
   so shunned the gown and flying cork.

Of late we've felt the touch of age
    and found the saddle pretty hard:
Our ponies, too, have lost the stride
    that once they had when tough and young;
So now we ride the printed page
    instead of round the caviayard,
To pick a top-horse here and there—
    the bronco songs that men have sung.

Oh, bronco songs that pitch and squeal
    and thrill the heart that pulses red!
Oh, mountain dawn and desert night
    and tinkle of the pack-horse bell!
The belted thigh, the roweled heel,
    the unregenerate hope that led
Our eager feet along the trail we loved so long—
    and love so well!

Old-timers in an ingle-nook we sit
    and drowse beside the flame;
We've stuck together through it all,
    and dream we live it all again.
We read the book and read the book
    and in our hearts we play the game,
And monument the sunset-trail for those
    who love the songs of men.

# It Was Overland the Red

"If you're askin' my opinion, well . . ." said Overland the Red,
    As he rose to do the honors, "I might say
You are takin' lengthy chances on what's goin' to be said;
    it's nothin' new—but put a different way.

"So I drink to California, the loved, the last, the best;
    To her women and her horses and her men;
To old El Camino Real windin' gray and lazy to the west,
    Loafin' up the range and loafin' down again.

"I drink to California, the land of the light and the gold;
    To the poppies noddin' happy in the sun;
To the snow upon the mountains layin' bright and white and cold;
    To the old trails and the trails that just begun.

"To the buckaroos a-ridin' out across the old Tejon;
    To the mules a-jinglin' lively down the grade;
To the herder squatted smokin' by his little shack alone;
    And the mockin'-birds a-dreamin' in the shade.

"To the girls that know a saddle from a pancake, on a hoss;
    To the desert-rat with 'color' on the brain;
To the rushin' of the rivers that no man has learned to boss
    When the ridges shed the roarin' winter rain.

"I drink to California, the darling of the West;
    To her women and her horses and her men;
A blessin' on those livin' here and God help all the rest;
    . . . In concludin' . . . we'll stand up and drink again."

# The Hills

Shall I leave the hills, the high, far hills
   That shadow the morning plain?
Shall I leave the desert sand and sage
    that gleams in the winter rain?
Shall I leave the ragged bridle-trail
    to ride in the city street—
To snatch a song from the printed word,
Or sit at a master's feet?

To barter the sting of the mountain wind
    for the choking fog and smoke?
To barter the song of the mountain stream
    for the babble of the city folk?
To lose my grip on the god I know
    and fumble among the creeds?
Oh rocks and pines of the high, far hills,
Hear the lisp of the valley reeds!

# The Desert

'T was the lean coyote told me,
    baring his slavish soul,
As I counted the ribs of my dead cayuse
    and cursed at the desert sky
The tale of the upland rider's fate,
    while I dug in the water-hole
For a taste, a drop of the bitter seep;
    but the water-hole was dry.

"He came," said the lean coyote,
    "and cursed as his pony fell,
And he counted his pony's ribs aloud;
    yea, even as you have done;
He raved as he ripped at the clay-red sand
    like an imp for the pit of hell,
Shriveled with thirst for a thousand years
    and cravin' a drop—just one."

"His name?" I asked; and he answered,
    yawning to hide a grin;
"His name is writ on the prison-roll
    and many a place beside;
And last he scribbled it on the sand
    with a finger seared and thin,
And I watched his face as he spelled it out
    and laughed, as I laughed, and died.

"And thus," said the lean coyote,
    "his need is the hungry's feast,
And mine." I fumbled and pulled my gun
    and emptied it wild and fast,
But one of the crazy shots went home
    and silenced the waiting beast;
There lay the shape of the Liar, dead;
    'twas I that should laugh the last.

Laugh? Nay, now I would write my name
    as the upland rider wrote.
Write? What need? For before my eyes
    was a wide and wavering line;
I saw the trace of a written word
    and letter by letter float
Into the mist as the world grew dark;
    and I knew that the name was mine.

Dreams and visions within the dream;
    turmoil and fire and pain;
Hands that proffered a brimming cup,
    empty ere I could take;
Then the burst of a thunder-head;
    rain! It was rude fierce rain!
Blindly down to the hole I crept,
    shivering, drenched, awake!

Dawn; and I saw the red-rimmed sun
    scattering golden flame,
As stumbling down to the water-hole
    came the horse that I thought was dead!
But never a sign of the other beast
    nor the trace of a rider's name;
Just a rain-washed track and an empty gun;
    and the old home trail ahead.

# Sunshine Over Yuma

Sun down the road where once the range,
    Unfenced, rolled sweeping like the seas,
Now gray now green the grassy change,
    Wind-swept and wavering languorously.

Sun down the road and gentle kine
    Shuffling along a hometown lane,
Where once the cowboy rode the line,
    Captain of herd and hill and plain.

Listen! In dim Valhalla he
    Flings past the milling phantom steers,
Chanting, in ghostly revelry,
    The sprightly spirit of his years:

"Come my little cayuse and lope along, lope along,
    Don't you go to start a little row!
You mustn't go to buckin' or to bitin' or to kickin';
    Don't interrupt the angels while their little harps they're pickin',
For we got to keep the rules or both of us will get a lickin';
    We're ridin' on the Big Range now."

"But there's not a single echo as you lope along, lope along;
    Not a single friend to answer 'How!'
There is sunshine over Yuma and the little owls are cryin';
    Red across the 'dobes strings of chills are a dryin';
But we're cinched to ride in Heaven, and that's what we get
      for dyin';
    We're ridin' on the Big Range now."

With lithe-limbed ease of poise and seat,
  With scarf of flame and starry spur,
Head up and proud he rides to meet
  The mighty throng that sway and stir;

Knight, Archer, Troubadour and Squire,
  Poet and Warrior, Prince and Peer
For gathering, mark his strange attire,
  Astounded at the song they hear:

"Come my little cayuse and lope along, lope along,
  We're headed for the Grand Pow-Wow!
But down in Arizona there's a Chola girl a-waitin';
  There's sunshine over Yuma where the mocking-birds
    are matin';
Oh, Glory is a mighty lonely trail—this navigatin'
  All around the Big Range now."

"So come my little cayuse and lope along, lope along;
  Guess we got in wrong, somehow.
Don't exactly fancy just the way the folks are starin';
  Can't exactly cotton to the funny clothes they're wearin';
Oh, it's heaven, but it's lonely, and we've had our little airin',
  So we'll fan it back to Arizona now."

# A Bronco Shod With Wings

Sing me a home beyond the stars,
    and if the song be fair,
I'll dwell awhile with melody—
    as long as mortal dare,
But sing me to the earth again
    on wide, descending wings,
That I may not forget the touch
    of homely human things.

Nor let my heart forget a friend,
    or turn from daily toil,
Though scant the measured recompense,
    the meal, the wine, the oil;
Nor scorn the rugged way I came
    with hunger pressing hard,
Before I knew the narrow gate
    or feared the breaking-yard.

The ragged coat, the grinning shoe,
    the glance bereft of pride,
And would I dare, who trod the mire,
    to thrust their plaint aside?
My dog's affection chides my soul
    for that I may not be
One half the loyal gentleman
    his eyes have mirrored me.

The homely things, the human things,
   the things, begat of earth,
And least among them
   he who scorns the clay that gave him birth;
My horse that nickers in the field
   and points his slender ears,
Has taught me more of gratitude
   than all the singing years.

What friends the trees, the soil,
   the stone, the turning grain, the flower!
House timber, garden, portal-step,
   bread, fruit, and fragrant hour
When shred, the leaf is touched by fire,
   draws cool and clear and clean,
And smoky spirals sing the praise
   of soothing nicotine!

The intimate companionship
   of saddle, spur, and gun,
The joy of leather, smooth and strong,
   of silver in the sun,
The grip of trout-rod to the hand,
   the play of jeweled reel,
The stock that fits the shoulder-curve—
   the potency of steel!

Forgetting not the rope and hitch,
   the steaming pack-horse train,
The sliding shale, the ragged pitch,
   the thunder and the rain,
The smell of coffee in the dawn
   that gilds the far divide;
Sing me a home beyond the stars—
   but give me trails to ride.

And so my friend, because, my friend,
    our ways lie far apart,
And I may never grip your hand,
    yet I may reach your heart:
I'll drop the reins and slip the cinch,
    untie the saddle-strings,
And carve a picture on the rock—
    a bronco shod with wings.

# The Lone Red Rock

A song of the range, an old-time song,
    To the patter of pony's feet,
That he used to sing as we rode along,
    In the hush of the noonday heat:

"Follow me out where the cattle graze,
    Where the morning shadows fall,
On the far, dim trails of the outland ways
    That lead through the chaparral."

There, where the red butte stands alone,
    And the brush dies down to sand,
Is the name of a friend—a mound of stone,
    And the sweep of this lonesome land.

His name is there, and a word or two
    And the brand that we used to run;
But his name could never mean much to you,
    And the old, glad days are done.

"Follow me out where the free sons ride,
    Where the young coyotes play,
Where the call of the quail from the mountain-side
    Comes out of the morning gray."

"Follow me out"—a laugh, a word,
    In the dust of the roundup, when
his horse went down in the milling herd,
    A break in the haze—and then;

I dragged him free, and he tried to smile,
    But his gaze was dim with Night;
"I'll rest by the butte a little while . . . "
    And the bronze of his face went white.

So a singer rode in the sunlit space,
    Past yucca and ridge and stone,
And a shadow with him, pace for pace,
    His own, yet not his own.

# The Far and Lonely Hill

Over on the Malibu
    we rode the range together;
Three as lively buckaroos
    as ever forked a hoss;
Playin' jokes and singin' songs in
    every kind of weather,
And anything we tackled—
    why, it had to come across.

*Sage a-shinin' in the rain;*
    *sun just breakin' cover;*
*Tail-to-wind the ponies*
    *standin' thoughtful—like and still,*
*While across the mornin'*
    *comes the cheepin' of the plover*
*Hidin' in the shadow*
    *of the far and lonely hill.*

Funny, how we never saw
    that it was drawin' nearer;
Edgin' closer every day
    that lonely hill it came;
Walkin' in the sunshine
    We could see it big and clear
But we kept a-ridin' and a-singin'
    just the same.

Little owls a-lookin' back
   solemn-like and blinkin';
Sunlight dancin' on the sand
   And burnin' out the grass:
Summer. . . round the water-hole
   the crowdin' steers all drinkin',
Just before we push 'em
   to the range beyond the pass.

Seems we didn't sing so much;
   ropes they did the singin';
Ponies' feet they played the tune;
   other riders told
All the yarns and sprung the jokes
   and kept the laugh a-ringin'.
Even then we didn't know
   that we was growin' old.

Two of us was left to ride
   the Malibu together;
And sittin' by the fire at night
   so solemn-like and still,
We began to notice
   every little change of weather,
Shiverin' in the shadow
   of the far and lonely hill.

Knew we had to climb it—
    knew the trail was mighty narrow;
Made a hand-shake on it
    that the next to go that way
Would kind of blaze the turns
    with our old brand "The Double-Arrow,"
So the last to follow
    wouldn't lose the trail and stray.

Down below I see the herd
    and dust a-rollin' higher;
Mornin' on the Malibu
    where once we used to ride;
Pony's frettin' on the bit—
    we can't go any higher;
I reckon if we got to go,
    it's down the other side.

*Sage a-shinin' in the sun that 's*
    *just a-breakin' cover;*
*All around the ranges*
    *loomin' high and cold and still,*
*As from the Other Valley*
    *comes the cheepin' of the plover,*
*And I see the Double-Arrow*
    *pointin' down the lonely hill.*

# Last of the Cavaliers

Nevermore shall the ranges ring
    as once when ye loped along:
Only the timid echoes sing
    old memories of your song;
Now what need that ye ride the line
    numb in the winter snow?
Fallen the far-seen upland pine;
    fenced are the plains below.

Out where the lone coyote shrills,
    limned on the desert sand,
Under the moon of the eastern hills
    baring that ghostly land,
Gleams the rim of the water-hole,
    white, with no print of hoof;
Ye would not know that yon shadowed knoll
    is the ridge of a nester's roof.

Still in Sonora's market-place
    gather the laughing girls,
Each a rose in the ebon lace
    filming her dusky curls;
Gay serape and eyes alight
    with the glint of a southern pride
Born of a kiss in the summer night:
    wondering where ye ride.

Ye rode singing down a thousand trails,
   drifting from change to change,
Dreaming of where the eagle sails
   over the open range;
Proud, ye held to your heart's desire
   scorning the newer years,
Lost in the glow of the sunset fire. . .
   last of the Cavaliers.

So ye went to your unknown end,
   answering jest with jest,
Recking naught where the trail might wend,
   men of the Golden West,
Spurring a rein-loose race with Chance,
   riding it hard and straight,
Living, unguessed, the True Romance—
   daring to love and hate.

*Have ye dreamed of the mesa grass*
   *starred with the flower of blue;*
*Morning haze in the mountain-pass,*
   *sage in the silver dew?*
*Blush of the mazanita bloom,*
   *bud of the almond tree,*
*Yucca hid in the canyon gloom;*
   *drone of the questioning bee?*

Now and ye ride in the sunset glow
   e'en as ye did of old,
Twain and twain as ye used to go,
   brave in the flare of gold,
Each his law; and all unamazed,
   facing the phantom plains,
Foot clear home and an arm upraised
   to the music of bridle reins!

# Riders of the Stars

Twenty abreast down the Golden Street
    ten thousand riders marched;
  Bow-legged boys in their swinging chaps,
    all clumsily keeping time;
  And the Angel Host to the lone, last ghost
    their delicate eyebrows arched
As the swaggering sons of the open range
    drew up to the Throne Sublime.

Gaunt and grizzled, a Texas man
    from out of the concourse strode,
  And doffed his hat with a rude, rough grace,
    then lifted his eagle head;
  The sunlit air on his silvered hair
    and the bronze of his visage glowed;
"Marster, the boys have a talk to make
    on the things up here," he said.

A hush ran over the waiting throng
    as the Cherubim replied:
"He that readeth the hearts of men
    He deemeth your challenge strange,
Though He long hath known that ye crave your own,
    that ye would not walk but ride.
Oh, restless sons of the ancient earth,
    ye men of the open range!"

Then warily spake the Texas man:
    "A petition and no complaint
We here present, if the Law allows
    and the Marster He thinks it fit;
We-all agree to the things that be,
    but we're longing for things that ain't,
So we took a vote and we made a plan
    and here is the plan we writ:—

*"Give us a range and our horses and ropes;*
    *open the Pearly Gate,*
*And turn us loose in the unfenced blue*
    *riding the sunset rounds,*
*Hunting each stray in the Milky Way*
    *and running the Rancho straight;*
*Not crowding the dogie stars too much*
    *on their way to the bedding-grounds.*

*"Maverick comets that's running wild,*
    *we'll rope 'em and brand 'em fair,*
*So they'll quit stampeding the starry herd*
    *and scaring the folks below,*
*And we'll save 'em prime for the round-up time*
    *and we riders 'll all be there,*
*Ready and willing to do our work*
    *as we did in the long ago.*

*"We've studied the Ancient Landmarks,*
    *Sir; Taurus, the Bear, and Mars,*
*And Venus a-smiling across the west*
    *as bright as the burning coal,*
*Plain to guide as we punchers ride*
    *night-herding the little stars,*
*With Saturn's rings for our home corral*
    *and the Dipper our water-hole.*

*"Here, we have nothing to do but yarn*
  *of the days that have long gone by,*
*And our singing it doesn't fit in up here,*
  *though we tried it for old-time's sake;*
*Our hands are itching to swing a rope*
  *and our legs are stiff; that's why*
*We ask you, Marster, to turn us loose—*
  *just give us an even break!"*

Then the Lord He spake to the Cherubim,
  and this was His kindly word:
"He that keepeth the threefold keys
  shall open and let them go;
Turn these men to their work again
  to ride with the starry herd;
My glory sings in the toil they crave;
  'tis their right. I would have it so."

Have you heard in the starlit dusk
  of eve when the lone coyotes roam,
The *Yip! Yip! Yip!* of a hunting-cry,
  and the echo that shrilled afar,
As you listened still on a desert hill
  and gazed at the twinkling dome,
And a viewless rider swept the sky
  on the trail of a shooting star?

# The Lost Range

Only a few of us understood
    his ways and his outfit queer,
His saddle horse and his pack-horse,
    as lean as a winter steer,
As he rode alone on the mesa,
    intent on his endless quest,
Old Tom Bright of the Pecos,
    a ghost of the vanished West.

His gaze was fixed on the spaces;
    he never had much to say
As he jogged from the Rio Grande
    to the pueblo of Santa Fe
He favored the open country
    with its reaches clean and wide,
And called it his "sagebrush garden—
    the only place left to ride."

He scorned new methods and manners,
    and stock that was under fence,
He had seen the last of the open range,
    yet he kept up the old pretense;
Though age made his blue eyes water,
    his humor was always dry:
"Me, I'm huntin' the Lost Range,
    down yonder, against the sky."

That's what he'd say when we hailed him
    as we met him along the trail,
Out from the old pueblo,
    packing some rancher's mail,
In the heat of the upland summer,
    in the chill of the thin-spread snow. . .
Any of us would have staked him,
    but Tom wouldn't have it so.

He made you think of an eagle
    caged up for the folks to see,
Dreaming of crags and sunshine
    and glories that used to be:
Some folks said he was loco—
    too lazy to work for pay,
But we old timers knew better,
    for Tom wasn't built that way.

He'd work till he got a grub-stake;
    then drift, and he'd make his fire,
And camp on the open mesa,
    as far as he could from wire:
Tarp and sogun and skillet,
    saddle and rope and gun . . . .
And that is the way they found him,
    asleep in the noonday sun.

They were running a line for fences
    surveying to subdivide,
And open the land for homesteads—
    "The only place left to ride."
But Tom he had beat them to it,
    he had crossed to The Other Side.

The coroner picked his jury—
    and a livery-horse apiece,
Not forgetting some shovels—
    and we rode to the Buckman lease,
Rolled Tom up in his slicker,
    and each of us said, "So-long."
Then somebody touched my elbow
    and asked for an old-time song.

Tom wasn't strong for parsons—
    so we didn't observe the rules,
But four of us sang, "Little Dogies,"
    all cryin'—we gray-haired fools:
Wishing that Tom could hear it
    and know we were standing by,
Wishing him luck on the Lost Range,
    down yonder, against the sky.

# Make Me No Grave

Make me no grave within that quiet place
    Where friends shall sadly view the grassy mound,
Politely solemn for a little space,
    As though the spirit slept beneath the ground.

For me no sorrow, nor the hopeless tear;
    No chant, no prayer, no tender eulogy:
I may be laughing with the gods—while here
    You weep alone. Then make no grave for me

But lay me where the pines, austere and tall,
    Sing in the wind that sweeps across the West:
Where night, imperious, sets her coronal
    Of silver stars upon the mountain crest.

Where dawn, rejoicing, rises from the deep,
    And Life, rejoicing, rises with the dawn:
Mark not the spot upon the sunny steep,
    For with the morning light I shall be gone.

Far trails await me; valleys vast and still,
    Vistas undreamed of, canyon-guarded streams,
Lowland and range, fair meadow, flower-girt hill,
    Forests enchanted, filled with magic dreams.

And I shall find brave comrades on the way:
    None shall be lonely in adventuring,
For each a chosen task to round the day,
    New glories to amaze, new songs to sing.

Loud swells the wind along the mountain-side,
    High burns the sun, unfettered swings the sea,
Clear gleam the trails whereon the vanished ride,
    Life calls to life: then make no grave for me!

# Alphabetical Index of Poems